PARTICLES

OF

FAITH

"*Particles of Faith* is the perfect book for our time. Stacy Trasancos explains the most fascinating concepts of science in terms that anyone can understand. She cracks open the treasure chest of wonders we encounter as we examine science through the lens of faith."

Jennifer Fulwiler
Catholic radio host and author of *Something Other than God*

"Many believers today feel caught between two seemingly contradictory worlds: that of their Christian faith and that of rational science. Stacy Trasancos precisely and methodically presents the harmony she has found. *Particles of Faith* will no doubt be a gift to the more scientifically minded who mistakenly think they must check their brain at the door of the church."

Rev. Dave Dwyer
Executive Director
Busted Halo Ministries

"Among many people today it's presumed that faith and science are at odds. We are encouraged to choose between the objective facts of biology or physics and the comforting pieties of religion. But, in *Particles of Faith*, Stacy Trasancos shows why this is a false choice through her own personal story as a scientist and a Catholic. She navigates many controversial touch-points between faith and religion such as cosmology, evolution, and quantum mechanics to reveal how science is supportive of the Catholic faith. Give this book to an atheist friend or any Catholic curious about whether faith can stand alongside science."

Brandon Vogt
Catholic author, blogger, speaker, and
content director of Word on Fire Catholic Ministries

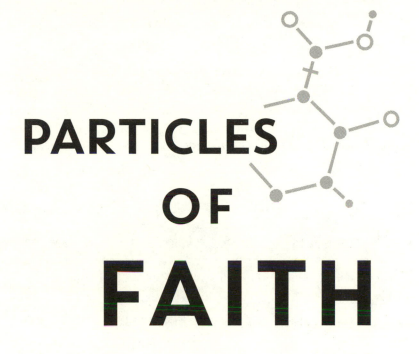

PARTICLES

OF

FAITH

A Catholic Guide to Navigating Science

STACY A. TRASANCOS

AVE MARIA PRESS AVE Notre Dame, Indiana

Scripture quotations are taken from *The Holy Bible, Douay-Rheims Version*, which is in the public domain.

Founded in 1865, Ave Maria Press is a ministry of the United States Province of Holy Cross.

www.avemariapress.com

Paperback: ISBN-13 978-1-59471-657-7

E-book: ISBN-13 978-1-59471-658-4

Cover and text design by Andy Wagoner.

Printed and bound in the United States of America.

Library of Congress Cataloging-in-Publication Data
Names: Trasancos, Stacy A., author.
Title: A Catholic guide to navigating science / Stacy A. Trasancos.
Description: Notre Dame, Indiana : Ave Maria Press, 2016. | Includes
   bibliographical references.
Identifiers: LCCN 2016021631 (print) | LCCN 2016023833 (ebook) | ISBN
   9781594716577 (pbk.) | ISBN 9781594716584 (Ebook)
Subjects: LCSH: Religion and science. | Catholic Church--Doctrines.
Classification: LCC BX1795.S35 T73 2016 (print) | LCC BX1795.S35 (ebook) |
   DDC 261.5/5--dc23
LC record available at https://lccn.loc.gov/2016021631

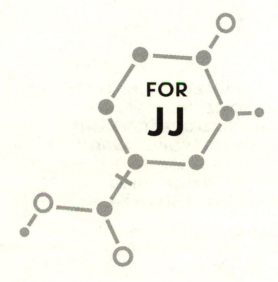

FOR JJ

FAITH BROADENS THE
HORIZONS OF REASON
TO SHED GREATER LIGHT
ON THE WORLD WHICH
DISCLOSES ITSELF
TO SCIENTIFIC
INVESTIGATION.

–Pope Francis, *The Light of Faith*

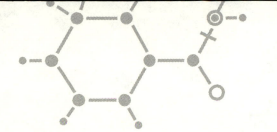

CONTENTS

PREFACE

I dedicate this book to my young son, José Jacinto Trasancos—JJ for short—because ever since he heard me say everything is made of atoms, he sees the world as atoms. "Mom, am I eating atoms? Are those trees atoms? Move! I need to pee atoms!" I did not realize what a thorough materialist I am until he expressed it so simply. Electrons and photons will blow his mind.

But I owe this book to Fr. Stanley L. Jaki. His book *The Savior of Science* was the first theology book I read in my first theology course after leaving a scientific career to raise children. I read it with a newborn JJ in my arms. JJ is a special gift: two children died in miscarriage before him and three after. My resolve to achieve a theology degree was a search for truth—to know what makes us human and where we go after we die.

When I read in Fr. Jaki's thesis that modern science was born from the nurturing womb of Christianity after being stillborn in other ancient cultures, the language resonated with me on many levels. Fr. Jaki was a physicist, a theologian, and a historian. I tried to contact him, but he died the year before JJ was born. I continued to study his works and three years later wrote a thesis titled *Science Was Born of Christianity: The Teaching of Fr. Stanley L. Jaki.* My purpose in this book is to bring Fr. Jaki's teaching to a new generation, and to breathe my own breath into his thoughts. May he, and JJ's closest siblings, rest in peace.

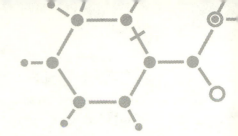

ACKNOWLEDGMENTS

I have been blessed with friends and mentors who are concerned about the faith-and-science dialogue of the future. I thank Dr. Walter Bruning for sharing his knowledge of physical chemistry, his love of the Catholic faith, and the occasional upbraid to keep me on track. He and his wife, Joanne, have stocked my library amply. I thank Ed Mulholland and Joel Whitaker for offering insight on the manuscript. I thank Fr. Mark Reilly for his friendship. He visits my family's remote home, prays with us, and provides direction in my writing endeavors. I thank Mr. Antonio Giovanni Colombo for checking for errors. I am very grateful for guidance from Dr. Jeff McLeod, faculty member at the University of St. Thomas in St. Paul, Minnesota, where he teaches at the St. Paul Seminary in the Archbishop Harry J. Flynn Catechetical Institute. He is a mentor who shines a light down the road. I would like to thank Dr. Stephen Barr from the Department of Physics and Astronomy at the University of Delaware for his helpful criticism of my summary of particle physics and explanation of free will. Special thanks to Dr. Christopher Baglow, professor of Dogmatic Theology at Notre Dame Seminary, for his direction in regard to the proper theological language.

I am grateful for the team at Ave Maria Press, particularly Fr. Terry Ehrman, C.S.C., for philosophical and theological guidance; Christina Nichols, for copyediting; Stephanie Sibal, for publicity; and Jonathan Ryan, for asking me in 2014 about writing this book and for steering me through this process.

I am most grateful to my husband, Jose, and children, Regan, Max, Abigail, Grace, Marie, Lucy, and JJ, for being the purpose in my life.

Everything is for you—to love you and to help you feel more at home in this world God has given us.

INTRODUCTION

ONLY A SCIENTIFIC MEMOIR

I want to explain first of all that this is not a memoir of my full religious conversion. When I tell stories about my scientific experiences, I use them to explain why I have the perspective that I do and how I navigated certain difficult questions after I became Catholic, to give you something concrete to remember as you talk with friends, family, and interlocutors on the topic of faith and science. Catholics are challenged to give answers whenever some controversy over faith and science erupts in our culture. I never knew there was such a controversy until after I converted to Catholicism and began to be challenged by atheists, other Christians, and other Catholics. This is a memoir, if you want to call it that, of how I navigated science in the light of newfound faith. It is meant as a guide for fellow Catholics.

This book is not a scholarly apologetic work either, because there are ample good scholarly works on faith and science already. I could have made the points in a more aseptic style, but it would not reflect either the way I think or the way I communicate with friends and family on the Internet and around my kitchen table. I notice something missing in the faith-and-science dialogue, and that something is the human person. Science involves people. Faith involves people. Whatever challenges and controversies arise, they arise because of people. Therefore, I seek to show how a Catholic *person* works through these questions of faith and science.

My experiences qualify me for commentary on the encounter between faith and science. I worked as a doctoral student in academia and as a research scientist in the global chemical industry for a total of ten years, and I was nonreligious during that entire time.

The whole story is best left for another time. I envision writing those memoirs when I am ninety years old, rocking in my old wooden chair on the porch, martini in hand, finally able to call the story complete. For now, suffice it to say that I searched anew for truth at around age thirty-three, and God granted me a love for life, an appreciation for the gift of children, and a blow of humility. I left my career to better care for my two children and entered the Catholic Church three years later. In my first seven years at home, my husband and I welcomed five more children in quick succession.

Theology studies helped my brain survive the interminable hours of nursing, feeding, changing, washing, and rocking babies. At first I could not fathom how anyone could add any new knowledge in a field that was built on articles of faith. Theology seemed like an exercise in word games. I soon discovered that the study of theology is a convert scientist's dream. The Church hands down the fiduciary knowledge of divine revelation from scripture and tradition. The task of Catholic theologians is to communicate this knowledge to contemporaries and help deepen their understanding of it. I found out that theology is science, the highest science. Any question I could think to ask about the Catholic faith, I could find logically addressed in Church documents, in the same way I once found answers to questions about scientific research in the rows of scientific journals in university libraries.

The science of theology is about ultimate purpose, whereas what we call science today is limited to the physical realm. My studies lifted me, you could say, above the terrain that bound me so that I could finally see the bigger picture, one in which science was properly situated as part of a greater truth, but was not itself the full truth. As this higher vantage of science in the light of faith was coming into focus intellectually, my days as a mother forced me to stay in touch with our humanity. I literally earned a master's degree in dogmatic theology through an Avogadro's number of diaper changes, sippy-cup refills, sister-fight breakups, and piles of unsorted laundry.

Eventually my training as a scientist, my education as a theologian, and my experience as a mother united into a concern for others who are navigating these confusing times—times when science is spoken of as omniscience and faith is regarded as a void for the mushy-minded. What I have to say is not profound; it is rather simple. It is a plea to fellow Catholics to return to that childlike awe and wonder with an unwavering confidence in Christ and his Church when we approach the subject of modern science.

NEVER AN ATHEIST

The second thing I want to make clear is that I never called myself atheist. It is incorrect to say that I am an atheist-to-Catholic convert. I guess I was a "None" before Nones were called Nones: I am a convert from nonreligiousness. I did not want to go to any churches, and I did not want to deal with any questions of any gods because I had no desire to join any of those social clubs. Perhaps I could never deny a belief in God even though I rejected religion. Perhaps I was lazy in not picking a side.

I knew some atheists, and they made atheism seem a sort of strange religion unto itself. There is a big difference between "nonreligious" and "antireligious." The former committed me to nothing. The latter would have committed me to tenets and dogmas I was willing neither to fight for nor to fight against. Outspoken atheists seemed to me like fight pickers, like the boyfriend who breaks up with the girl but will not stop calling her to remind her. Why label yourself with a word derived from something you do not believe in or want to be associated with?

As a research chemist, I knew many people from plenty of different cultural backgrounds and religious convictions. Even in the years I was nonreligious, I did not disrespect or despise the religious people I knew, for that would have been petty and rude, the behavior of an insecure person. In hindsight, I realize it was my scientific training that protected me from such bigotry because scientific training teaches you to withhold judgment until you have gathered empirical evidence. And I converted precisely *because* I gathered enough empirical evidence and arrived at a sound conclusion.

I admired the integrity and work ethic of many of my religious colleagues, particularly the Catholic ones. No proselytizing swayed me when I was ready to take the leap of faith. On the contrary, part of my empirical evidence came from observing how they lived their lives. They possessed something special, a deep and pervasive confidence. I let myself hope that I could attain that confidence too.

SYSTEMATIC THINKING

Third, I want to address my mode of thinking and communicating. I am fond of systematic thinking, of placing definitive points of knowledge into the broader picture. For example, if you bake bread, you may focus on exactly the right amount of yeast to use, and you may test different quantities over time to discover how it affects your product, but you work the details out in service of the greater systematic context of sustenance, enjoyment, and communion. Everyone engages in systematic thinking, but not enough emphasis is put on it in education.

I first learned systematic thinking as a scientist. You research the background, narrow in on the questions that need more investigation, conduct your experiments, analyze your data, and then situate your results and conclusions back into the greater context. I was fortunate that my training as a chemist was broad: I did polymer, electro, physical, quantum, bio, analytical, and organic chemistry. That breadth had everything to do with my doctoral advisor, Thomas E. Mallouk at the Pennsylvania State University (Penn State). In my 1999 dissertation, I thanked him for teaching me how to think, and a decade and a half later his instruction continues to serve me well, even though I no longer do chemical research (except in my kitchen).

When I thought systematically as a scientist, however, I still limited my thinking to science. Studying philosophy and theology showed me how to systematize science into the universal picture. When I say "science in the light of faith," I refer to such broad, authentic systematic thinking.

In this book, I steer through these questions: What is the relationship between faith and science? How do you sift through scientific conclusions? Does the Big Bang prove God? Is the atomic world the real world? Does quantum mechanics explain free will? Did we evolve from atoms? Are creationism and intelligent design correct? Can a Christian accept the theory of evolution? When does a human life begin?

Part 1 of the book is devoted to the general relationship between faith and science. Part 2 navigates some of the challenging questions posed by physics to faith and by faith to physics. Part 3 deals with the big questions posed in the biological sciences and how we navigate them without compromising our human dignity or faith.

I cite the works of individuals throughout the book because, as I said, science, faith, and any conflicts between the two involve people. The views of groups or opposing sides are best understood by exploring what individuals mean when they pose arguments. I try to put together what I think a person new to the dialogue needs to get started. If I say, "I think" or "in my opinion," I do not mean to weaken my point but to indicate that I am aware there are other opinions.

Now, I want to begin by telling part of my story.

PART I

SCIENCE IN THE LIGHT OF FAITH

CHAPTER 1

A STORY ABOUT THE CHASM

FAITH OF A CHILD

Some people say children are born atheists, but I have no recollection of ever making any decision not to believe in a higher power. My earliest memories were naturally of God, of being awed by perfection and vastness beyond me and beyond us all. I grew up in rural Texas during a time when running barefoot in the woods, making mud pies, catching grasshoppers, and hunkering down in a ditch for hours because Bigfoot was surely after us were all as natural to a kid as breathing air.

The skies are bigger than imagination in Texas. Whether in the moonlight or the noonlight, a girl can lie on her back and see into the void of the sky, registering with her eyes the colors and shapes of nature but completely unable to register in her mind what lies between, beyond, and behind the visible things of the world. I remember thinking of the stars as memories because I read that light took years to reach our eyes and that the stars we see may no longer exist.

Like any fortunate kid, I had hope. I regarded each new day as an opportunity to experiment with my surroundings. I knew that no matter how much I played with dirt, handled bugs, examined clouds, and tried to count leaves on trees, even if I did it for the rest of my life, I would never explore everything.

Perhaps nostalgia colors those experiences more joyful than they really were, for I was not an easygoing child, but sometimes I wish it were possible to see memories the way we see stars. The first memory I would see would be my mother's face as I looked up from her embrace.

When she told me God made the trees, the big, round sun, and me, my fascination was fueled by the thought that God made everything. Children start out assuming there is a unifying logic to it all. *To a child, faith and science go hand in hand.*

In high school I learned the chemical reactions of the Krebs cycle (also known as the citric acid cycle or the tricarboxylic acid cycle), and it was a formative event. The Krebs cycle is a series of chemical reactions used by aerobic organisms to generate energy for other metabolic pathways, and it is where most carbohydrates, fatty acids, and amino acids are oxidized to generate molecules to make other biological molecules. In this cycle, eight different enzymes catalyze organic reactions, beginning with citrate synthase catalyzing the condensation of acetyl coenzyme A and oxaloacetate to yield citrate. Students are expected to memorize exacting biosynthesis reactions, and I remember wondering, *Where did this brilliant machinery come from?* Science textbooks do not address that question. Nevertheless, when I looked up at a tree for the first time after coming to understand that these crazy, precise reactions are popping away inside every cell, the realization was overwhelming.

Within plants, invisibly and faithfully, sunlight is being converted into chemical energy by the process of photosynthesis to fuel their own activities, and glucose is being produced to provide energy for our bodies and oxygen for us to breathe; as if it were all planned out and designed that way. As complicated as it is, the Krebs cycle is but the hub of the overall process in which plants acquire and use energy to carry out the various functions of life. Plants are, in turn, the hub of the overall process in which organisms acquire and use energy to carry out the various functions of their lives. Life on Earth is interconnected in very precise ways at the atomic level.

The huge idea of biological machinery, our bodies included, was breathtaking. I could not fathom how other scientists ever figured all of that out. I could not fathom how the Krebs cycle, photosynthesis at large, even a single living tree, let alone a forest, the globe, or humanity and the universe, ever came to be. I wanted to know more, and my love for science, born in childhood, became manifest in adolescence.

LOSING MY RELIGION

Somewhere in my teen years, I let go of that childhood awe and won-der. Losing my appreciation of the perfection beyond me, I became obsessed with being perfect. When you are young and pondering the big, immediate question of what you might wear that day or what you might do after high school, you tend to care less about big-sky myster-ies and more about how you measure up, the right permed hair and big bangs, the right eyeshadow and lipstick, the right miniskirts and leg warmers, the right Jordache designer jeans, and even the right college courses so as to impress.

In college I majored in biology, and for the first time ever I flatly rejected religion, actually in the same year (1991) REM produced the song "Losing My Religion." I know that my interpretation is not what the song was supposed to be about, but words are words, and if you sing them enough, you make their meaning your own. Religion did not fit my style. If religious people wanted to eat yellowish casseroles at potluck socials, highlight their study Bibles, practice for choir con-certs, and believe the "Old Rugged Cross" would save them by "Amaz-ing Grace," worms that they were, so be it. Religion was not for me. I wanted to learn how the world works. I wanted to see the world, and I wanted to be somebody.

I reluctantly took a teaching job three years into my undergradu-ate studies; the university worked out an agreement with a high school that needed a chemistry teacher, and it was hard to argue against grad-uating early for a job if you were going to college to get a job. So I bought some black suits, got an apartment, and taught high-school chemistry in Athens, Texas. On the first day of class, when I had to say the names of my first students out loud to call roll, I froze like a kid hiding in a ditch again, sure Bigfoot was about to get me. I was twenty-two and mortified that I was not much of an authority figure. I did it, though. I learned how to lead, think on my feet, and explain complex subjects to a variety of people.

There was another benefit: I had to review the basics of chemis-try. Looking back, I can see that reviewing and teaching high-school chemistry made me own the material in a fundamental and personal way. The trajectory of a science career usually does not involve a return to high-school fundamentals, but the time I spent teaching chemistry in my early twenties undoubtedly cemented concepts in my mind that otherwise would have remained vague.

In spite of all I gained from teaching, I knew that repeating the basics year after year for the rest of my life would not be enough. My fascination with biological machinery was full-blown by then because I had been reading Ayn Rand's *The Fountainhead* and *Atlas Shrugged*. I also found myself portrayed in Albert Einstein's writings. In a collection of his notes about science and religion titled *The World As I See It*, Einstein wrote that "in this materialistic age of ours the serious scientific workers are the only profoundly religious people."[1] Yes, that was me—a serious scientific worker in a lab coat with an angled face and simple but coiffed hair (like Rand's female protagonists might look). I knew I would not contribute to the field of chemistry or biology if I remained a high-school teacher for the rest of my career. So, two years after starting that role, I wrote a rather hubristic letter of resignation to the high-school superintendent informing her that I was like a machine, a fine automobile in fact, in need of fine-tuning to reach my fullest potential. In order to make that happen, I announced, I was going to leave teaching to pursue a doctorate in chemistry. The superintendent may have been impressed with my resignation. I cannot say. Anyway, I went back to school.

SAVING THE PLANET

I returned to my original university to complete a set of courses in undergraduate chemistry to prepare for graduate school, so I had some time to plan. By then, I had developed the skill of, and fallen in love with, reading scientific literature and scientific papers. I was able to devour them because solidifying my understanding of the fundamentals of chemistry had given me the ability to understand the importance of the papers. I could understand the background of different projects, and it excited me to read how scientists around the world were literally reaching into the unknown to provide humanity with new knowledge about the machinery of the universe. I wanted to be part of the action, and my reading told me I needed to know what I wanted to work on before I applied to graduate schools.

To me, reading scientific literature was like reading fashion magazines must have been to some other young women. I dreamed of publishing papers. Scientific papers in refereed journals are where researchers meticulously present their most recent work in so much detail it is almost like being in the laboratory with them. A college library is full of volumes, often dating back decades if not half a century, detailing scientific discovery—the closest thing you can find to the "magisterium of science," so to speak. I spent much time in the university library, and of course I dressed the part. I traded the black suits for something more poetic: an ironed, button-down, white shirt, worn jeans tucked in tall boots, and wild hair, kind of like Julia Roberts in the movie *Flatliners*. I worked myself up about saving the planet, the buzzword "nanotechnology," and not being a cog in the wheel.

In those mid-1990s days, the headlines were full of reports about how the greenhouse effect, acid rain, and holes in the ozone were going to decimate the rain forests and kill off many species of animals, the ever-increasing human population included. In addition to reading scientific literature, I picked up a few popular science books to gain a vision of the future. Jonathan Weiner's 1990 book *The Next One Hundred Years: Shaping the Fate of Our Living Earth* affected me most.[2]

I was never one to get involved in scientific arguments about the fate of our world, as that seemed an unreasonably mammoth-sized problem to solve. It seemed more effective, following some of the suggestions in Weiner's book, to focus on what I could *do* rather than say. I could boycott anything with chlorofluorocarbons, and boy did I try. I even gave up hairspray and tried to grow dreadlocks to make a statement against aerosols, but after two months all I had was one giant knot of hair in the back of my head that had to be cut off. I could recycle, and I did, but back then we did not have the efficient recycling collection systems we have now, so I had to store my recycling until I could drive it to a recycling center (which upset me because driving was bad for the planet) and it caused my apartment to become infested with roaches from all the empty food containers stored in the pantry. I could stop eating meat, and I did so without much pain by substituting more chocolate and cheese into my diet. The unfruitful lifestyle efforts aside, my main takeaway from Weiner's book was that my generation had to do something to develop new energy sources to slow down the emission of carbon dioxide into the atmosphere. I set out to do my part there too.

Weiner's book explains there are three gases that best act like a greenhouse's glass walls and hold heat in our atmosphere. These three "greenhouse gases" are water vapor, carbon dioxide, and ozone, and they share a feature that oxygen gas and nitrogen gas do not have: their molecules are composed of three atoms instead of two. Having three atoms gives these greenhouse gases the special property of trapping heat. When the sun shines on the Earth, high-energy radiation passes through these three-atom molecules to the ground where the radiation is converted into lower energy heat (thermal, also called infrared) radiation. The heat rising back off the ground does not pass back through these molecules. Instead the infrared radiation is absorbed by the bonds in these greenhouse gases. The absorbed energy causes the bonds to vibrate and release more infrared radiation, which is absorbed by other nearby greenhouse gas molecules. Hence, the heat is retained in our atmosphere rather than released back out into space.[3]

This greenhouse effect is related to the cycling of the seasons. Plants take in carbon dioxide during the spring and summer when they are green and the sun is shining on them; via photosynthesis, they convert the sunlight into chemical energy, which synthesizes the carbon dioxide and water into carbohydrates (which store the energy) and oxygen (which we breathe). When the leaves wither and fall to the ground or become food, the carbohydrates decompose back into water and carbon dioxide, so the plants give back some of the carbon they took from the air. This is called respiration. The planet can be thought of as (although we know it is not) an organism inhaling and exhaling (breathing) carbon dioxide throughout the processes of photosynthesis and respiration.

Scientist Charles David Keeling charted the change in concentration of carbon dioxide in Earth's atmosphere starting in 1958, and the data is still gathered today even though Keeling died in 2005. In his book, Weiner explains that these plots are evidence that the buildup of carbon dioxide in the atmosphere would "change the breathing of the world."[4] Technological optimists, he says, interpret changes in the Keeling plots as evidence that the world is breathing more deeply; technological pessimists see the Earth getting out of breath, gasping.

Having grown frustrated with hairdos, rotting pizza boxes stashed in my gas-guzzling Ford Fairmont, and the few pounds I put on as a chocolate-and-cheese-consuming vegetarian, I decided I needed to do something more than spin like a cog in the wheel of a culture strangling the planet, and I knew it had to be something visionary. The chapter in which Weiner discusses the gasping planet and the Keeling curves begins with a quote that is highlighted in yellow in the copy of his book that still sits on my shelf, for I treasure it along with the other books that shaped me: "So it cometh often to pass, that mean and small things discover great, better than great can discover the small: and therefore Aristotle noteth well, 'that the nature of every thing is best seen in its smallest portions.'"[5]

I had no idea who Aristotle or Francis Bacon were, nor did I care, but the words "the nature of every thing is best seen in its smallest portions" resonated with my mechanical worldview. It hit me then that if we humans wanted to *do* something that would save the planet in the long term, we—I—needed to study and simulate what plants do. I needed to simulate photosynthesis, and to do that I needed to learn how to manipulate atoms.

I read K. Eric Drexler and Chris Peterson's 1991 book *Unbounding the Future: The Nanotechnology Revolution*, and my visionary path uncoiled before me.[6] This book is a tour of all the ways nanotechnology—the ability to manipulate matter at the atomic level—can improve our lives and save our planet. Particularly, Drexler discusses how molecular manufacturing can provide clean solar energy by mimicking photosynthesis. Materials could be used more sparingly than in human-scale technologies, and pollutants could be minimal and more controllable since the machines would be molecular. As machines grew more perfect at the molecular level, their motors, bearings, insulation, and computers could become less wasteful. Molecular machines could, like plants and the chemical cycles that sustain them, produce waste products that are the reactants for the next cycle of production. Nanotechnology, he says, could be the "ultimate recycling technology."[7] I knew that if I could get into a research lab that simulated photosynthesis on nanomaterials for the purpose of providing new energy sources, I could become more than just someone who lived in her time and place and did what the wheel of her culture made her do. I could become a mover. I could help save the planet.

So I put down the popular science books and headed to the library to sift through science journals for the latest research on using nanotechnology to create artificial photosynthesis. The subject spans several disciplines: physics, biochemistry, materials chemistry, and polymer chemistry. I learned of a research team that had just recently moved from the University of Texas at Austin to Penn State and was researching, among other things, artificial photosynthesis on nanometer-scale inorganic particles with a long-term goal of producing new materials that could, like plants, take energy from the sun and convert it into chemical energy. In 1993, I wrote to Dr. Thomas E. Mallouk's Chemistry of Nanoscale Inorganic Material Research Group at Penn State. He invited me to visit the university; I was accepted into the graduate school with the customary full scholarship plus stipend, and the following fall I moved 1,200 miles northeast, away from my family and the big skies of Texas, to pursue my dream of becoming a serious scientist.

WRESTLING WITH NATURE

My first assignment in the Mallouk lab at Penn State was to work with Dr. Steven Keller, the postdoctoral fellow who was conducting the research on artificial photosynthesis on inorganic-organic nanometer-scale composite assemblies. It is an understatement to say that I thought my life was complete, but I had in my mind only my *scientific* life, while I knew my personal life was a disaster and did not know how to unify both lives. By then, I had given birth to two children, but I was so beholden to my career that I was an absent mother. Scientific research makes it easy to put personal problems on the shelf because you have to block everything else out in order to do your work.

In my arrogant mind, I was the rare Randian, Einsteinian heroine doing necessary work. Everything else was secondary, including the two inorganic-organic highly complex multicomposite assemblies who called me mother. I actually referred to my children as "inorganic-organic highly complex multicomposite assemblies" on the day they sat in the front row at my doctoral dissertation defense; it is painful to recall how insensitive, full of myself, and lost I was.

My task was to learn from Dr. Keller, publish with him, and then continue the project with the team after he left the group to start his own career. For the most part, daily life in the lab was not about success. A chemistry professor told me early on in my scientific endeavors that if I wanted to become a research chemist, I had better be able to handle failure, by which he meant that the vast majority of my experiments would fail to do what I wanted them to do. He was right. We had enough good results with artificial photosynthesis to get articles published in the *Journal of the American Chemical Society*; the *Proceedings of the Robert A. Welch Conference on Chemical Research in Nanophase Chemistry*; an advanced textbook, *Photochemistry and Radiation Chemistry: Complementary Methods for the Study of Electron Transfer*; and the *Coordination Chemistry Reviews*.[8] I do not list those accomplishments so much to impress (although they were impressive to me) but to set the stage for my comeuppance.

What we did, while noteworthy enough to merit publication, was small—not small as in nanoscale, but small as in insignificant compared to what leaves actually do. In spite of all I was accomplishing, I still could not quite forget what I had known as a child to be true: our knowledge is a speck compared to our ignorance. I have a knack for missing the obvious, so I kept on wrestling.

We were trying to simulate a single electron excitation and transfer along the electron transport chain in the light reactions in the photosynthetic cycle. Let me back out from those reactions to put the process into the bigger perspective. Photosynthesis begins, of course, with sunlight; it occurs within a plant cell in organelles called chloroplasts.

Within the chloroplast there are thylakoid disks, the membrane of which contains pigment molecules, called chlorophyll, that absorb certain wavelengths of sunlight. When sunlight strikes a chlorophyll molecule, the energy of the light "excites" the electrons in the chlorophyll molecule.

If the molecule were isolated, in theory the excited electron would simply relax and emit radiation, but since the molecule is part of an orchestration of molecular machinery in a plant cell, the electron instead is transferred to another protein molecule, and then to another and another and another and so on, much as people might toss a hot potato down a line.

This electron transport chain in the thylakoid membrane is not random but highly organized. Each passing of the potato, so to speak, allows some energy to be lost, but the energy from the electrons is not wasted. The controlled release of energy can be used to convert adenosine diphosphate (ADP) into adenosine triphosphate (ATP) or to pump hydrogen ions into the thylakoid disk for other uses. These molecules are the solar batteries that keep life pumping. The result is that light energy from the sun is used to run much of the biological machinery on Earth. The electrons, whose journey we were following, are not wasted either. They are passed to a second transport chain where they continue to be productive. After that journey, the electrons still have energy, and are transferred to the stroma (the inner fluid) of the chloroplast by a molecule of nicotinamide adenine dinucleotide phosphate ($NADP^+$). The $NADP^+$ combines with a hydrogen ion and becomes NADPH, which goes on to play an important role in the production of carbohydrates.

The details go on and on, but the point is: open a biology textbook and look at the reactions in just the process of photosynthesis and tell yourself, "Leaves are doing this." Chloroplasts in leaves are precise and sophisticated nanomachines.

ONE PITIFUL JUMP

We were only trying to simulate one electron transfer. One. We were not trying to design an electron transfer chain. We were not trying to do anything useful with the energy or the electrons. We were merely trying to get excited electrons to jump from one molecule to another and stay there long enough to measure it.[9]

Our designs were intelligent for sure. We grew concentric mono-layers, roughly one molecule thick, of redox-active (able to accept and lose electrons) organic polymer layers on high-surface-area sil-ica particles. The silica particles were "fumed silica," a thickening agent typically used in cosmetics, paints, adhesives, and even cat litter. Fumed silica is commercially produced by vaporizing quartz sand in a >1500°C flame so that droplets of amorphous silica agglomerate into an extremely fine powder with a high surface area and irregular shape. We visualized our composite assemblies of polymers grown on these silica particles somewhat like lasagna noodles coated on squashes. In a typical procedure, we used five grams of silica particles, which amounts to about a fifth of an acre of surface area in a small test tube. The attention to detail is difficult to convey. Doing chemistry is a lot like cooking—but blindly, because the stuff you cook up occupies a realm invisible to the naked eye.

Someone had to synthesize the polymers (large molecules com-posed of many repeated subunits) in the first place; this was another postdoctoral fellow's work before I joined the team. Then the postdoc-toral fellow I worked with had to figure out how to determine whether the monolayers of polymers in fact grew on the silica particles. The only way to see those layers was to view the composites at steps along the way under a transmission electron microscope (TEM). The pro-cess of building the composites and analyzing them took weeks, and our final confirmation from the room-sized microscope that we had perhaps grown the lasagna layers on the silica squashes as we were trying to do was a TEM picture that looked something like a bunch of popcorn balls coated with caramel. We called it a "mottled coating." In other words, it took some hard staring to convince ourselves to pro-ceed with the next phase of the experiment—the attempt to simulate that one measly electron transfer.

That phase required going into the basement and setting up our sun—the second harmonic from an Nd:YAG laser that produced

532-nanometer light—so that it would hit a pinky-sized quartz cuvette of our polymer-coated silica particles and excite the electrons. Timing the laser flash, the mechanical shutters, and the optics can be compared to trying to thread a needle with a wet noodle behind your back using a mirror in the span of time it takes brain cells to tell your eyes to blink. I look back now and am amazed that we were crazy enough to think we could pull off even one pitiful jump.

We determined that our experiment worked. The photons of light excited the electrons, and we measured that about 30 percent of them transferred to another polymer layer, staying there for a half-life of about 21 microseconds. In other words, a third of our excited electrons jumped and stayed put, but only for a very small fraction of a second. Then, unlike the real electron transport in photosynthesis, they relaxed back to their initial ground state. In contrast, the many steps of the electron transport chain in real photosynthesis approach 100 percent quantum yield (excited to transferred electron ratio) and pass the electrons onward to do their before-mentioned work. To put our project into the context of the global picture, plants consume about six times more energy than the human race each year.

In truth, we artificial electron transfer groupies were but puny observers and manipulators of laws magnificently beyond the work of human hands, and we knew it.

OVERWHELMED BY NATURE'S SYMPHONY

You know how a single memory can get seared into your mind, an experience that you recognize only in retrospect as a turning point in your life (just as you cannot recognize a curve if you can see only two points because you are standing too close to it)? I will never forget the real metanoia (reorientation) in my intellectual life, although I did not recognize it as such on the day it happened. I did not understand it, actually, for another fifteen years. The life-changing event took place one day as I stared out a window from the third floor of Chandlee Laboratory at Penn State.

I had just spent hours trying to make sense of piles of data that took six months to collect; I had consulted a biochemistry text in case reviewing the chemical reactions of photosynthesis might shed some light on the jagged lines I was trying to interpret. My data looked like a kindergarten art project. I was starting to panic at the thought that my graduation would be delayed or, worse, not granted. As I stood at the window, gripping the ledge and trying to get a grip on myself, my eye fell on an old *Ginkgo biloba* tree peeking around the corner of the end of the building, a big tree I had never really noticed before. With trepidation, I fixated on the funny-shaped leaves. There were so many. And they flapped in the wind carelessly, mindlessly achieving what I never would.

Those leaves were converting photons of light into energy in nearly perfect quantum yield and passing electrons from one molecule to the next to do the necessary work of life, thousands of them on hundreds of erratic branches. Every square millimeter contained half a million or so of the chloroplasts that contain the molecular machinery for photosynthesis. Right there, so close, was an orchestration of photons, electrons, atoms, ions, molecules, organelles, leaves, branches—a tree so finely tuned down to the quantum level that it did not seem like it should exist. But photosynthesis has been playing longer than the human race has existed. That tree had existed longer than I had lived. Electrons whizzed away in my body even as I had that thought.

In that moment, I felt a great anxiety, or pain, or something. The best way I can describe the feeling is to compare it to the way I feel at orchestra concerts. As a child, I had the privilege of playing the violin with professional musicians in a university orchestra because my teacher was the lead violinist and instructor at the university. I once enjoyed music, but I became overly focused on technical details in my studies and overly stressed sitting on stage, always in proper concert full black, trying to keep up. I knew that every single instrument makes every note precisely tuned and timed. I knew there are nuances in the way lips have to be formed and lungs have to expand and exhale, in the way hands have to be held and feet have to be placed. As I got older, I learned that laws of physics could describe the motion of molecules moving under forces in the wood, metal, strings, and the sound waves vibrating through air; and mathematics could describe the notes and chords orchestrated in space and time. To this day, I do not know how anyone is supposed to relax as the music plays faster than a human can fully appreciate it. Maybe sadness is what I feel rather than pain or anxiety—in my limits, I cannot stop time and appreciate the music fully, for to stop time would end the music.

I had the same feeling staring out the window that day. I knew what that *Ginkgo biloba* was up to in its atomic proportions. I was at a concert, with unrelenting scores of notes passing my mortal ears, lost and gone forever, wasted. *My God, if only we could stop time I would hear every note in every layer in every beat from every player and give it its due because "the nature of every thing is best seen in its smallest portions."* I would see the atomic nature of the music and the tree, and I would appreciate it all.

That day, staring at that tree, I tried to appreciate the whole, but all I saw was a chasm. The tree might as well have been on one side of the Grand Canyon and I on the other being forced to face the fact that I would never measure up. The tree held the truth about nature, the truth that Someone made it, and it was frightening. Flinging myself out there to reach the truth made as much sense to me at the time as jumping off a cliff because everyone else did. There was no way I was going to jump because I had no idea what would happen next.

So I did the only thing I could do. I cursed the damned tree, hurled my pinky-sized vial of intelligently designed, artificial-photosynthesis, world-saving nanotechnologies, data included, into the metal trash can behind me, tightened my ponytail, and got back to work.

You see, a chemist is privileged to wrestle with the laws of nature, but that privilege delivers a blow of humility. I learned something my professor had not prepared me for. The 99 percent failure rate is not what burdens scientists, because scientists learn from failures; the burden comes from the knowledge that all of your research demands that you reach into a darkness hoping for the slightest glimmer of light. You know the truth is there beyond your reach, awaiting discovery, and you want so desperately to know what it is. For a scientist who does not believe in God or creation, there is an additional, monumental burden: you do not even know why the truths you are striving to discover are there; you have no fundamental explanation for why you care about science.

People hold scientists in such high regard as intellectuals, and it is true that the work is hard and requires much practiced skill. But what so much of the discourse about faith and science omits is that conducting scientific research does not instill in a person the broad knowledge traditionally associated with intellectuals. The work is more like grunt work at times. The intellectual aspect is brief and takes a budding scientist from broadly absorbing scientific literature in a specific area of research into narrower and narrower, exceedingly specialized scientific method cycles to hypothesize and test exceedingly specific questions. If you wanted to plot it, a scientist's knowledge looks like a vertical spike—scientists know very much about very little. Because their work is specialized, the normal mode of thinking for a scientist is to shelve questions that cannot immediately be explored, the same way people do not care to know how their smartphones work.

Turning around and getting back to work was not in the end all that hard. Sure, for a moment I could not help but wonder about the bigger question of where it all came from. I let myself glimpse the chasm between what we observe in nature and what we can do in a (then) state-of-the-art university research lab, but I could only face it briefly. In retrospect, I know that it was a moment of grace. Every day from then on I knew I worked on the edge of a precipice with my back to some unknown abyss of truth beyond science, and I learned to live with the knowledge in the same way I learned to practice my violin one note at a time and blend in with my black dresses. To turn around and deal with the chasm would have distracted me from my work, my minuscule single note in the symphony I was trying to play in.

SERENDIPITY

At any rate, during my time at Penn State, I was specifically charged with the project of building a polymer/silica assembly that would complete *two* electron transfer steps and another one that would pump protons like the machinery of photosynthesis does. I never got either to work. I never published as the primary author on an artificial photosynthesis project.

Serendipity saved my scientific career as it has saved many others. I had learned how to synthesize almost perfectly spherical 35-nanometer diameter silica nanoballs because we tried to grow the assemblies on more uniform surfaces. We thought we could achieve more uniform layers on uniform surfaces and hence have more success at electron and proton transfer. A colleague, Patti, and I had an almost humorous idea while strolling through an exhibit on campus one day. Someone had made a phenolic resin replica of a form by applying monomers (small molecules that can join together to form polymers) onto the surface, polymerizing (curing) them, and then dissolving the form away. This is an old industry procedure. The phenolic polymer is commonly known as Bakelite resin, and it has been used to cast forms such as pipes, fountain pens, cameras, and gun parts.

Patti looked at me and said, "We could do that on the silica balls." We came up with the idea to press the balls together into a pellet with a hydraulic press and then heat the pellet at a high temperature to sinter (fuse) the particles at their points of contact. You know how you can put a lot of gumballs in a jar and they naturally order themselves in an array? It is the same idea, but imagine that you also glue the balls together in place. Our pellet would thus have a porous three-dimensional structure, around which a monomer resin could be synthesized. Since the spaces between the fused balls were so small, on the nanometer scale, the trick was to get the molecules of monomer into the spaces between the nanoballs. We immersed the pellet in a solution of calculated concentration so enough monomer could flow into the voids, and then we heated the incorporated (coated) pellet overnight to cure the polymer, just as is done in industrial-scale production. We dissolved the silica balls away with hydrofluoric acid because we knew that acid dissolves glass, washed the remaining material with water to remove traces of the acid, and confirmed with elemental analysis that what was left was the phenolic resin we intended to make. TEM images confirmed that the resin had filled enough of the spaces to produce a replica in the form of a three-dimensional ordered porous array.

Prof. Mallouk was out of town when we first tried the synthesis, but when he returned, he put our fun into perspective and guided us to complete the project. We decided to get fancy and introduce a second monomer that would make the resin less rigid and somewhat "shrinkable" with heat. We could, therefore, "tune" the pore sizes by adjusting the ratio of the shrinkable polymer to the rigid polymer. We prepared TEM images of polymer replicas with precise 15–35-nanometer diameter pores. To our joy, the plot of monomer ratio to pore size was a nearly straight line. That alone was not convincing enough, so we also confirmed the pore volume with nitrogen adsorption techniques. Then, to show off, we made a silica replica of the resin replica and showed that it was ordered too.

We had just achieved the first preparation of three-dimensionally ordered, porous organic polymers from inorganic templates with a tunable crystalline pore network in the 10–50-nanometer size regime, ironically by invoking an old industrial process. We published similar techniques using other inorganic materials as templates in *Chemistry of Materials* and in *Journal of Materials Chemistry*, but the so-called "nanobubblepack" graced the pages of *Science* journal and a few popular science magazines.[10]

Publishing in *Science* journal is a big deal. *Science* only publishes the most significant original scientific research across all scientific disciplines and across the globe. The materials we prepared were said to have possible applications for the preparation of mesoscopic (larger than nanoscale) devices, such as ordered arrays of metal or semiconductor quantum particles, and for various sorption and separation processes involving biological macromolecules.

That 1999 *Science* paper has since been cited in ten or so textbooks about nanotechnology because our nanoscopic replicas were among emerging new techniques for ordered, three-dimensional porous materials. The accomplishment is nowhere near the notoriety of famous scientists, and I certainly do not intend to give that impression. But it is satisfying to know that we contributed new knowledge to the field of nanochemistry. I did not do much to save the planet in four years, but true to the words I left behind with the high-school superintendent back in Texas, I finely tuned something—I *did* something—even if it was only bubblepack for molecules.

Prof. Mallouk is the distinguished Evan Pugh University Professor of Chemistry, Physics, Biochemistry and Molecular Biology at Penn State, and he is the head of the Department of Chemistry. Still on the noble mission of providing energy solutions for the future, he is the director of the Center for Solar Nanomaterials, and I still follow his work. His army of chemists has grown considerably since I was in his lab, and I still benefit from the enthusiasm for the molecular realm that he inspired in me.

E. I. du Pont de Nemours offered Patti and me jobs upon our graduation. Penn State named us doctors of philosophy (PhD), a funny title for me if ever there was one, since the word "philosophy" made me either stare blankly into space or shudder. I accepted a position as a senior research chemist in the Lycra® business, where I helped develop new spandex formulations with my knowledge of polymer chemistry and inorganic additives—spandex, the stretchy stuff in pantyhose, swimsuits, t-shirts, jeans, and underwear. I liked to say that I was giving new meaning to the cliché "Spandex is a privilege, not a right." I worked in the very building where spandex was invented, with my own laboratory and office and with dominion over experimentation. I was quite the professional demigod in my hard hat, safety goggles, lab coat, and steel-toe boots. Every day when I arrived at work in my black Mazda Miata with my golf clubs stashed beside me in their hot pink bag, I felt I had arrived in life. Instead of saving the world, I traveled it.

Five years later I left my career because my new husband asked me how I defined success.

THE LEAP INTO THE CHASM OF FAITH

My husband's question helped me realize that my children needed a mother who did more than role-model research in a global industry, and I made the decision to leave my position as a chemist with finality. In a seniority-based system such as the one I worked in, walking away is permanent. I wondered if I was giving up everything I had achieved, but by then it was abundantly clear to me that science did not have all the answers. I do not mean to say that a working mother cannot give her children what they need, only that I failed to do so.

I was literally a science fideist, able to separate myself from everything else but my science, and I am still good at compartmentalizing my thoughts. I placed so much faith in the assurance that success as a scientist meant success in life that I merged myself with my scientific career and neglected my personal life, most importantly my children. So when I decided to turn around and investigate what is really important before it was too late, I had only one choice: I had to face the music. I had to face the chasm. I had to choose God, my husband, and my children, and to take the leap of faith. True to my chemist nature, I became a homemaker enthusiastic about bringing my talents to bear on the domestic enterprise awaiting my touch. I fancied myself a cook totally excited about concocting dishes in my in-house laboratory where I could manipulate atoms and serve them up to living and hungry analytical machines.

My husband suggested that I might find other interests besides chemistry.

And I did. Three years later I was received into the Catholic Church. Now I teach high-school, college, university, and seminary courses online for Catholic institutions, and I do it from home because home is where my husband and I raise and educate our youngest five children. I strive to inspire a love for creation in my students. When my students learn about atoms, I tell them to be amazed at the Creator who ordered all things. I tell them not to be disheartened because they do not know everything, but to embrace learning for their lifetimes. My teaching *is* my doing. I am not saving the planet, nor do I travel the world, but I am leading souls from my helm at home.

Today when people ask me if I would do it again, I know I would. Life is funny like that. When young women ask me if they should pursue science even if they might leave the career to raise a family, I encourage them to trust that they will make good decisions when the time comes. Time in graduate school or time in a short career is not time wasted. It shapes you, and you have the satisfaction of knowing you contributed new knowledge to a field of study. As I am discovering now that my children are getting older, education is never over. I am busier than ever working to further the dialogue between faith and science. I may have walked away from a career, but I found a vocation. Your choices are what you make of them. If you commit to excellence and to adding value—for the greater glory of God—you will always make contributions.

In a tangible way, I flung myself into the unknown, having no idea what the truth would demand of me, and I was afraid at first. It is similar to the way scientists delve into the natural unknown. The difference in digging into science is that you keep your feet on the ground and dig around to see what you can find. You do not take personal risks in the same way you take them when you accept faith.

Flinging yourself into the chasm of faith puts the very depths of your soul and life at risk, and you do not know if you will fall to the bottom or learn how to fly. I have discovered in that mysterious chasm the air of abundant grace, the "something special" I had seen in other Christians. Each morning I take long walks, pray the Rosary, and breathe in grace. Even with the demands of daily life, each day is like Christmas and Easter morning all wrapped up into one. As it turns out, the air of grace lifted me so I could see a larger landscape of reality, family, purpose, love, and of course, science. Granting assent to the articles of faith was the most intellectually satisfying leap I ever dared to take as a scientist and, more importantly, as a person. Now I see science as the study of the handiwork of God. And I see so much more.

We live in a wood cabin tucked away in the Adirondack Mountains surrounded by the grand, sophisticated machinery of thousands of—you guessed it—trees. Thanks to my husband, I am so immersed in a surrounding of created natural beauty that I have no choice but to let go and appreciate the symphonies of nature. Instead of pining for time to stop so I can analyze every detail, I have learned to live in the given moment, to appreciate the larger purpose of it all. Although I remain an incurable materialist, I now see atoms in the light of our Catholic Faith.

I have learned to reverse my shelving, to put the small questions aside and deal with the big questions. I have rediscovered my childhood sense of wonder. I still wear mostly black because it makes me feel like I blend in. My husband gave me a violin and a grand piano in case I wanted to take up music again for enjoyment. I learned to play "Ave Maria" on the piano. The violin remains in its case. All things in their time.

* * * * *

The threefold moral of the story is this:

1. If someone tells you that science has all the answers, try not to die laughing. Or if you prefer something more composed, repeat this line from the prologue of the Voet and Voet college-level *Biochemistry* textbook: "In all cases, our knowledge, extensive as it is, is dwarfed by our ignorance."[11] Or repeat this line from the end of the Walker, Haliday, and Resnick college-level *Fundamentals of Physics* textbook: "The main message of this book is that, although we know a lot about the physics of the world, grand mysteries remain."[12] I knew this as a child. I knew it as a research chemist. As a Catholic, I finally understand why we will never know everything. Life is exciting when you realize that you can spend all your days learning new things.

2. If a scientist is aware of the chasm, he or she must choose either to ignore it or to face it in the light of faith.

3. Every human is a wayfarer.

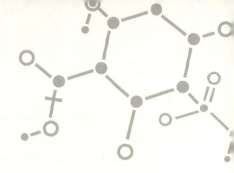

CHAPTER 2

ANALOGIES ABOUT HOW FAITH AND SCIENCE RELATE

THE BATTLESHIP OF SCIENTISM

Picture the opening crawl on a movie screen:

"A long time ago in a galaxy far, far away . . .

"It is a period of conflict. Out in the great darkness called Ignorance, the rebel Battleship of Scientism soars through space and time, and claims its victory against the old Reign of Religion.

"Today the sons and daughters of Scientism say they have the knowledge to save the universe. They perceive they are pursued by Religion's sinister agents, and they claim they race ahead in progress, while the followers of Religion, encumbered with their dogmas, fade into the darkness pleading that there is no conflict . . ."

And then we enter the story. The followers of Religion surge back into the scene, led by new leaders, and they fight to defeat, reclaim, or hang on to the Battleship of Scientism. Science exploded in their lifetimes and has provided insights into the way the world works and those insights have brought new technologies. At first, Science soared forward faster than people could keep up, and the people became confused and divided in their quest to stay relevant in the modern world.

Some followers of Religion now join the Creationist Sect, a group of fundamentalists who reject the Battleship of Scientism as an enemy because they do not trust it. They have their own version of Science based on a literal interpretation of the Bible. Presenting themselves as the sole authorities of both science and religion, these warriors shoot their arrows high and long from their ancient bows. Their mission is clear. They want to destroy the Battleship of Scientism before it destroys the Reign of Religion, but their arrows only ping the metal.

Then an Intelligent Design Army rises up. Their leaders are less dogmatic and fight with newly made weapons and tactics. They do not take aim from afar at the ship, but plan a different attack, to infiltrate the ship and sway the skeptics of religion using their own brand of scientific terms. The Intelligent Design Army writes a test for Intelligence thereby showing that the God of Religion (or perhaps the Alien King of another galaxy) is the Designer after all because, they say, "Science says so." Some of them issue propaganda: "See, Science makes the case for God." With each wave of attacks upon the doors of the Battleship, the occupants block the Intelligent Design Army and kick them off the ship, which the Intelligent Design Army finds most unfair.

Others try to cling to the battleship, and profess an allegiance to Science. These particular defenders of Religion fight to stay attached to the Battleship of Scientism, catching a ride on top, tying themselves on to sides. They even fly out in the periphery trying to keep up. They call the spacecraft the Battleship of *Theistic* Scientism to keep themselves inserted in the action. They fear that if they lose contact with Science, they will be left behind, forgotten, to float meaninglessly in that dreaded void of Ignorance, but their presence and their god-adjective irritates the ones flying the Battleship of Scientism.

Over time, people grow accustomed to the chases and the battles, and they lose sight of the unity that once actually existed between Religion and Science before the Battleship fired off in rebellion. The Creationist Sect, the Intelligent Design Army, and the Theistic Entourage tell themselves that they can once again be assured of their rightful place at the new frontiers opened up by Science because they have earned it with all their fighting. Amid the turmoil, there remains an unspoken fear that Religion may be destroyed by Science in the end. But for the moment, numb to the unstable influence of scientism on them, voices rise up, "There is no conflict here."

Intolerant of such firing, thieving, and clinging, the occupants of the Battleship of Scientism eventually increase their defenses and fire bullets at these false adherents of Science. "How can you know Science?" the Battleship people roar, "Your Religion is against Science. Leave us alone or submit to our rule! The Reign of Religion is over!" A great battle looms on the horizon because the Battleship of Scientism will not stray from its trajectory toward progress into the unknown. What their enemies do not know is that the pilots of the Battleship of Scientism have their own insecurities. The ones at the helm, dare it scarcely be said, have not a clue where they are going.

All of those caught up in the battles have lost sight of the way back to peace or the way forward to progress.

Still others have chosen to ignore the Battleship of Scientism almost completely because it has become imposing and intimidating, its language obscure. These people stay behind the battle and toil as they always have. To them, the occupants of the Battleship utter strange pronouncements about the universe, the nature of matter, and the meaning of life, so strange that they are not sure how to calmly challenge its pilots who pontificate their new views of the cosmos. These people live in peace, but they rely on others to bring boons from Science to their lands.

And yet, there are others. They identify with Religion and Science both, but do not form sects, armies, or thought squads. They uphold the legitimate Reign of Religion as a universal force for good, and while they fight mighty battles against dark forces, they do not chase after the Battleship of Scientism. Their work is to guide and protect in confidence and patience. These visionaries move about the lands and carry on true science, true civilization, true progress, at times behind the scenes, each doing his or her part, at other times as great leaders who rise above the fray, and at other times as martyrs willing to die for good rather than join evil. They see the Battleship of Scientism for what it is, a shiny fast-moving freewheeler that will not continue for long without assistance from those who can navigate the way forward.

These noble souls serve the people, but never without the clear vision gained from their raised perspective. Their faith broadens their horizons of reason, and allows them to shed greater light on the world that discloses itself to scientific investigation, but they know there is more to do than science. They are the network that binds the human race (or even alien races should they ever be found), and in the fullness of time, they will guide the Science Ship as a parent guides a prodigal child, no longer as a Battleship but as a vehicle illuminated by the light of faith and propelled steadily onward and upward, toward the end of time, leading people beyond to the final Kingdom. The leaders in black say, "Peace be with you."

It is our work here to put this phony Battleship of Scientism in the hangar and take a good look at it, to correct our image of the relationship between faith and science. In our time, we must deal with scientism as if it were indeed some fortress speeding into the future, but in reality science needs guidance from people of faith. What is scientism though? We need to examine that word.

For understanding the meanings of words, the *Oxford English Dictionary* (*OED*) is my favorite resource because it is a historical dictionary. The *OED* is regarded as the authority on the English language because each entry traces the history of a word from its origin to the present day so the reader can understand how people have used the word over time. It is a look into the collective mind of the past.

Of course "scientism" comes from the word "science," which derives from the Latin *scientia*, meaning "knowledge." Knowledge refers to understanding, learning, and erudition.[1] In the thirteenth century, St. Thomas Aquinas began his *Summa Theologiæ* by asking, in the very first questions, whether theology is a science—that is, a body of knowledge.[2] One objection was that there is no need of any science higher than the philosophical sciences because we cannot "know" what is above reason. Since the philosophical sciences go as far as reason can go, the objection goes, then philosophy is the highest science. St. Thomas argued that we must also study scripture and divine revelation, citing 2 Timothy 3:16: "All Scripture, inspired of God, is profitable to teach, to reprove, to correct, to instruct in justice." In that sense, when we study scripture and divine revelation, we gain knowledge of it. Furthermore, when we study scripture, we see what has been revealed by God and is, therefore, not accessible purely by reason. Theology is a science inspired by God and whose object is God, therefore, theology is the highest science. It is doubtful that many would claim theology as a science today, much less the highest science, but St. Thomas's explanation brings us back to the broader definition of science and its unity with theology.

Since Aquinas's lifetime during the thirteenth century and onward as the medieval universities became established up into the fifteenth century, the meaning of *scientia* evolved, focusing down from "knowing and understanding" to "learning in a particular area of knowledge, such as a recognized branch of learning or discipline."[3] The medieval Catholic universities specifically defined the seven subjects for study—the seven liberal arts—that form the *trivium* (grammar, logic, and rhetoric) and the *quadrivium* (arithmetic, geometry, music, and astronomy).[4] The four subjects of the *quadrivium* were called mathematical sciences. Theology and other areas of learning, including research into the mysteries of nature, were understood to be organically linked.

Likewise, it was understood, particularly by St. Albert and his student, St. Thomas, that different disciplines had their own autonomy and way of conducting themselves to answer their own questions. Eventually, science came to be contrasted with art. Art was thought of as a discipline or field of study as well, but as a practical application of knowledge.[5] Those who practiced a trade of a skilled nature, or a craft, were artisans. Their arts were achieved or mastered by the application of specialized skills.

Starting from the sixteenth century, scholars accumulated knowledge of how mathematics can describe the physical laws of nature. This rise in mathematical understanding of the natural world in the sixteenth and seventeenth centuries is taken as the scientific revolution, which encompassed rapid and far-reaching developments into new branches of knowledge, such as physics, biology, and chemistry. These new discoveries of physical laws fundamentally changed the way people viewed nature and their place in the cosmos. Old ways of gaining knowledge gave way to wide-ranging and fascinating new ways, and this new knowledge had a great impact on European intellectual culture.

Excitement over the new understanding of the physical world expanded, perhaps too rapidly and without checks, leading to the virulent scientism of today that we need to define. "Scientism" is the belief that only knowledge obtained from scientific research is valid, and beliefs deriving from religion should be discounted. It is an extreme or excessive faith in science or scientists.[6] It is a rebellion battleship that represents something good and useful—science—but has been piloted by people who have lost sight of its origin or its future. We need to see science for what it is, but we do not need to chase after the battleship trying to destroy science or cling to it just because its pilots are overzealous. We need to be ready to guide science in the light of faith.

If you are young and interested in science, I want to tell you something that you will not hear many people say. *The scientific community needs you.* They need leaders who will work among them with a confident vision of the benefits that science can bring to humanity and with a humble fortitude to lead the way. Not only must you refuse to set your faith aside as a scientist, you must strive to think systematically, to keep the larger picture in view even as you become an expert on the technical details. The scientific community needs visionary people of prayer and hope, people who are unafraid of truth, goodness, and beauty. If you are not young, but interested in science, you have a role in this story too. Help inspire our next heroes.

Looking back at history, I think the excitement over modern science is understandable. There is not much point in railing against the past. It is better to understand the past so we can influence the present and future. Somewhere along the way, knowledge gained by reason came to be regarded as more certain than belief in God, largely because of the rise of science. Let us continue our investigation of a few more words that affect how we think.

Medieval philosophers made a clear distinction between knowledge gained by reason and that gained by belief, as in "certain belief." "Belief" in the religious sense traditionally meant having sure knowledge based on an intellectual assent of faith.[7] Belief meant more than merely having an opinion. For Christians, belief meant the assurance of the existence and faithfulness of God and an acceptance of the teachings of the Catholic Church, the trust one places in God, the Christian theological virtue of faith. It is the virtue of granting assent to things unseen, of striving to reach what is beyond human nature, and of believing in God and what he has revealed.

According to the *OED*, the word "scientism" was first used in the late nineteenth century to refer to the method of conducting modern science, not at all a depreciative word. But that word changed from a method to a belief, in a lesser sense of the word than people of faith use it. Recall the definition of modern scientism; it is the *belief* that only knowledge obtained from scientific research is valid.

The confusion is a rather simple one to clarify if we rely on definitions. The pilots of the Battleship of Scientism have a "belief," but they do not really understand what it means to have a belief. We do not need to destroy them. We do not need to fight them. We need to be firm in our faith—our belief in Christianity—and be ready to guide them as guardians of truth, to be able to recognize legitimate scientific progress and to reject any claims that overstep the bounds of science.

In the seventeenth century, philosopher and scientist René Descartes published his work *Discourse on the Method of Rightly Conducting the Reason, and Seeking Truth in the Sciences.* The full title highlights the excitement over physics in Descartes's time. Descartes wrote in part 4 that the laws of physics he had thus far discovered were a highly useful knowledge distinct from the "speculative philosophy" taught in schools.[8] He saw physics as practical because by knowing the "force and action of fire, water, air, the stars, the heavens, and all the other bodies that surround us" people might apply them just as artisans apply their knowledge of arts. But he went further. He wrote that knowledge of physics would allow us to "render ourselves the lords and possessors of nature." In the context of this statement, he was arguing for using learning in physics to advance learning in medicine and to improve people's lives, which is admirable. Still, the "lords of nature" language affected how people viewed the power of science.

It became a widely held view that metaphysical or philosophical learning was not a suitable method for acquiring new knowledge, and this distinction led to the separation of the physical sciences from the

philosophical and metaphysical sciences. Francis Bacon, a contemporary of Descartes, showed this evolution in thinking in his *The New
Organon or: True Directions Concerning the Interpretation of Nature*. He
wrote in the preface: "In short, let there be one discipline for cultivat-
ing the knowledge we have, and another for discovering new knowledge."[9] Perhaps he did not intend it, but this is the divide that has
continued into our time, promoted by the empiricism of others from
the sixteenth to eighteenth centuries, including Thomas Hobbes, John
Locke, Baruch Spinoza, and David Hume. Empiricism is the idea that
knowledge comes only from sensory experience, and the logical conclusion of strict empiricism is that the scientific method is the only
method suitable for the search for truth.

As with any discussion of history, it is impossible to treat the rise
of scientism fully because modern scholars are limited to looking back,
reading texts, and trying to figure out what people meant. They must
sift through the historical record for the bits that tell the story they are
trying to tell, and they are limited to examining the texts left behind.
Our purpose is to make sure we understand where scientism came
from. I do not think it is much of a stretch to say that many, if not
most, people who have been affected by scientism do not know it has
a name and do not know its history. But to understand a little of the
history of scientism is to understand how to avoid being taken in by it.

Here is a test to see if you are at risk for unwittingly succumbing
to the rampant scientism of today, by which I do not mean that you
are embracing scientism or intentionally promoting it, but only that its
effects have seeped into your thinking as they once seeped into mine.

*What is the first thing you would say if someone asked you about the
relationship between faith and science?*

Would your first reaction be to point out that faithful people can
also be people who love science? To assert that many Catholics were
scientists as evidence that even Catholics can do science? To point to
this or that conclusion in science as an example that science supports
faith?

If so, stop and examine those reactions. Why does a person of faith
need to defend his or her ability to love science or to be reasonable?

Why single out that Catholics can be scientists? Of course we are reasonable, and of course we can be scientists! Why point to any particular scientific conclusion as if it could prove the existence of God? We hold religious truths in faith and certainty because they are revealed by God, not because scientists give them the nod.

Underneath your response, is there a fear that faith might be unreasonable?

Faith, that substance of things hoped for and evidence of things that appear not (Heb 11:1), is ultimately not just the stuff of physical quantification. Do you have a concern that faith and science might actually conflict, that evolution, for example, might disprove the foundational dogma of original sin, or that physics might prove that matter does not follow laws of nature? That science explains everything people once thought faith explained? Is there a fear that you will have to pick a side? If you admit that you sometimes wonder about these questions, do not worry. You are not alone. I have been there. I have talked to people, young and not so young, who have been there and are still there. It is understandable. So many opinions are bounced around by people who think their opinion is the only right one. It is no wonder people end up feeling as if they should stay out of the way lest they unintentionally put their faith at risk.

So let us right the imagery. Wherever you fit into the caricatures of the Battleship of Scientism story (and they are extreme caricatures), stop and stand back far enough until you find that you admire science, for it does indeed cut through ignorance and drives progress. If you stand back far enough, however, you will notice that scientific discovery does not actually fire forward in a straight line. When viewed from a broad enough perspective, discoveries and theories appear to meander. The history of science is full of twists and turns, false starts, and explosive spurts, some of which turn out to be false starts anyway. If you look broadly enough, you will see that modern science emanates from, and is sustained by, the light of faith. Faith in an ordered world is the reason we do science. In fact, science was born in a Christian culture on purpose, a history tied to the biblical Old Testament, which we will cover in more detail when we cover Fr. Jaki's work in chapter 4. For now, let us discuss a less dramatic analogy.

AN ENDURING FRIENDSHIP

One of the most useful analogies I have ever read about the historical divide between faith and science is given by Dr. Christopher Baglow in his book *Faith, Science, and Reason: Theology on the Cutting Edge*. He tells a story about new rumors and old friendships.[10]

Suppose you move to a new town, and on the first day you arrive, the town is abuzz with the news that Susie and Johnny hate each other.

"Oh, those two! They will never reconcile. They are so different! How can they ever be friends? Those two should just go their separate ways and make sure their lives never overlap again."

Now, since you entered the history of Susie and Johnny when you did, you might take all those comments to mean that Susie and Johnny are truly enemies with irreconcilable differences. What you do not know, however, is that they have been friends since childhood. Their friendship is not over, and their lives actually overlap in significant ways. They had a fight, which was one tiff among many others that have forged their relationship over its history. However, in the current skirmish, people picked sides and falsely escalated the account. The chatter made Susie and Johnny's relationship sound like something it was actually not.

If you keep in mind that faith and science have shared dialogue over the millennia much more than people today make it seem, then you begin to have a solid grasp of the true nature of the relationship. The work of Fr. Stanley Jaki helped me understand that science and Christianity are united by a bond even stronger than friendship. His historical research shows how the biblical worldview gave rise to and guarded a correct view of the cosmos, the one that ushered in modern science.

This unity was affirmed in modern times by the encyclical promulgated by St. John Paul II in 1998, *Fides et Ratio*. His argument, in my opinion, is not that people of faith can be people of reason, as if that question is even valid. Rather, as its first heading says, the encyclical is about knowing ourselves. St. John Paul II tells us why we need both. He begins with the often quoted statement, "Faith and reason are like two wings on which the human spirit rises to the contemplation of truth" (*Fides et Ratio*, Blessing). He takes it as a given that we cannot reach our fullest potential without both.

The idea that faith is separated from, or subject to, reason has arisen relatively recently, due mostly to the fast advance of science and to the "exaggerated rationalism of certain thinkers" (*Fides et Ratio*, 45). This explanation ties into the previous discussion about the rise of scientism; the more the rationalists rejected faith, the more the faithful rejected rationalism, and mistrust grew. This is not a true divide or an old divide. It is a perceived divide in the imaginations of those who do not realize the history of the matter: that in medieval thought there was "in both theory and practice a profound unity" between faith and reason (*Fides et Ratio*, 45).

In order to pursue mystery, we need faith that something greater lies beyond ourselves, and by reaching into mystery, we discover more truth. It is a cycle. Reason alone is not enough. Faith alone is not enough. We need both to be fully human. The purpose of *Fides et Ratio* was not to point out how reasonable Christians can be if they so choose, but rather to show how much reasonable people need faith and faithful people need reason.

AND THESE THY ATOMS—THE STORY OF A MEAL

The correct metaphor, I henceforth propose, for understanding the relationship between faith and science is beautifully demonstrated in the way Catholics bless our meals: "Bless us, O Lord, and these Thy gifts." Meals are scientific feats. They are productions of innovation synthesized by the manipulation of matter in various chemical and physical changes orchestrated to serve up something good for humanity. The harmony of faith and science is the harmony of blessings and meals.

People of faith see a meal as a gift from God, from the bubbly cheese on top of a pizza down to every atom and subatomic particle in the bread dough. Atheists will not give thanks to God for a pizza or any other meal. They do not see atoms as the handiwork of God, but—and this is the cool part—diverse groups of people can still appreciate pizza together in the communion of friendship. This fact reveals something radical about the relationship between faith and science: *science can be the very venue through which we reach out into the world and shine our faith to illuminate the path to truth.* Sure, some people cannot be reached, but I know from my own experiences that Christians can radiate their light even when they do not realize other people are watching.

God made the nonreligious for truth and mystery too. Without those elements in our lives, we are not satisfied. Sundered from faith in God, people tend to cling to science because science provides at least some answers and some enigmas. Think about how the "Bless us, O Lord" understanding of faith and science could change the dialogue. We do not point to pizza and say, "See there! That is proof that God exists." When we bless our meals, we *start* with firm belief and it should be the same when we learn about or conduct science. Pope Francis said that faith is born of love and reflects God's own love (*Lumen Fidei*, 50). For those who have accepted it, faith draws us out into the world to build a place where we can dwell together.

I believe discussions about faith and science should take place in such a hospitable atmosphere. This spirit is the same spirit St. John Paul II instilled in the Pontifical Academy of Sciences. The academy invites scientists of all faiths, or of no faith, from around the world to gather into working groups to present papers and compare findings, knowing they will not provide all the answers. Science *should* unite us like that because we all agree that the material realm exists. Maybe the nonbeliever will not thank God for the mysteries and wonders of nature. Maybe the one of another faith will view the world differently or pray differently. But for Christians, science is a way of knowing God better through the study of his handiwork. Our faith can light the entire discussion. I have seen both sides, and this is my main message in this book. We have to tell people what science is in the bigger system of reality.

Allow me to stop right here and tell you how this idea came to me. We had some friends over who were not religious, friends we had only begun to get to know. They brought dessert. We cooked burgers. Our children played, ran, and ate cookies. The adults snacked on cheese and drank wine. All that physical stuff was good, but the most enjoyable part of the gathering was that we talked and laughed for hours. We bonded around our table. There was something about the intimacy of the setting—a trust, a mutual understanding that each of us was genuinely interested in the others. We wished to open our lives to each other, if only for an evening, and that turned into other gatherings and deeper conversations and lasting friendship. The material aspect was great, but the immaterial truth of a new friendship was even greater.

My husband and I never set our faith aside that evening or afterward. We prayed before the meal as we always do. Our home remained adorned with crucifixes and statues. When we spoke, we spoke as people of faith. That is how it should be when Catholics talk about science, and it really is that simple. As Pope Francis said, "Far from making us inflexible, the security of faith sets us on a journey; it enables witness and dialogue with all" (*Lumen Fidei*, 34). The lesson here is this: If (1) faith illuminates the encounter with science, then (2) faith comes first. (3) Never, ever upend that order. We need faith and reason equally, but when it comes to science, we must view the universe through a confident lens of faith in the Creator.

Later, when my son JJ heard me say that everything is made of atoms, he wanted to know if he was eating atoms, and of course, I enthusiastically agreed that he was. He put the idea of "science in the light of faith" into words during our blessing: "Bless us, O Lord, and these Thy atoms." Leave it to a child.

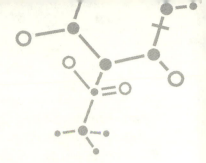

CHAPTER 3

NAVIGATING SCIENCE IN THE LIGHT OF FAITH

THE RIGHT OUTLOOK

How many times do we hear of teens or young adults who delve into science and decide to reject their faith because, they say, they are choosing reason over faith? Time and again science gives conclusions that seem to contradict tenets of Christian faith. Some of us might feel consternation or even panic at that thought. What do we do if a scientist says science proves that something we hold in faith is wrong? How do we respond? How do we know whom to believe? Can you imagine how it must have felt to the people of Galileo's time to have their worldview challenged? Probably you can, because there are similar issues in our times.

Today we wonder about evolution, cosmic origins, the mind, and the soul. It might help to recollect the worldview in Galileo's time. Catholics believed the universe was created by God with a beginning in time. That view was not wrong, but it was incomplete. Finding out that the celestial realm is made of the same kind of matter as earth challenged what the people understood about natural science, but the truth they claimed that God created the heaven and the earth was untouched. They were right to maintain faith that God created a celestial realm beyond our imaginations, but they were wrong about how it existed. They were right to maintain that humans are special in the hierarchy of creatures, but they were wrong to think the Earth is the center of the universe. Galileo himself was not completely right, and since his time our understanding has grown—thanks to the efforts of scientists, mathematicians, philosophers, and theologians.

Faith and science are two different manifestations of the same reality. When they seem to have conflicting conclusions, it is because our knowledge is not complete.

People tell me I am a sort of walking contradiction because I have studied both a field of physical science and theology, but there are a lot of people like me outside the realm of the media. I know a lot of scientists who are Catholic, many of them priests, and they are living testaments to the unity of faith and science.

Atheists have wanted to know how a scientist could make a choice to be a person of faith and embrace belief in a personal God. They wonder how I could shift from relying on empirical evidence as a scientist to ordering my whole life around the articles of faith. They ask me how I can accept something as true that I cannot prove in a laboratory, and I understand what they mean. I understand how strange faith looks from their perspective.

What they do not realize is that I *did* gather qualitative empirical evidence in the sense that I made observations and formed conclusions based on experiences. I tested the tenets of faith in my life laboratory, and I found them to be true. For example, I obeyed the obligation to attend Mass on Sundays and holy days of obligation, to pray daily, to honor my role as wife and mother, to pursue virtue, and to try to avoid sin. Choosing to do those things clarified the truth I could not see when I was unwilling to enter the laboratory to experiment. When atheists criticize faith, it is as though they are standing in the hallway of a laboratory criticizing the scientists inside, whose work they do not understand. The empirical evidence I gathered gave me confidence that the leap of faith was a leap into truth.

The exercise of living a life of faith is actually not all that different from the exercise of learning about atoms. When I first wanted to learn about particles, I trusted the fiduciary knowledge passed down by scientists, instructors, and authors. I memorized and studied until I owned the knowledge about the invisible realm of chemistry. I decided that I believed atoms existed, and my tests confirmed that the laws I learned were able to predict outcomes. If I calculated, based on the atomic weights on the periodic table, how many moles (6.02×10^{23} molecules) of an acid would neutralize a base, for example, I could perform a titration and verify that it worked.

Other Christians have asked me how I reconciled what I knew about science with what I learned about faith. They wanted to know how I sorted it all out. The answer is that I did not sort it all out, but I figured out how to navigate the issues.

The difference between navigating and calling the journey complete derives from the fundamental understanding that the knowledge we gain in our lives will never be complete. We are rational, intelligent beings, but we must rely on our senses to take input from the world before we can make abstractions and theories about how it works—hence the scientific method.

There is a natural tendency to dive into a new question feeling either anxiousness to find the right answers or the temptation to dismiss the question because the information seems hidden behind technical language. Try to temper both extremes. Learning is difficult if you are not clear about what you know and do not know, and there is no shame in admitting limits. Truly, it is an intellectual virtue to be honest about the limits of your knowledge, and it is quite liberating and clarifying. When you are new to a question, write down what you understand, try to articulate what you think you grasp, and pinpoint precisely where you begin to be confused.

Then, do not rush to form an opinion. The most controversial topics involving science and religion are debated because there are no clear answers. Learn what is known about science, but remember that science is provisional. A "provision" is something that supplies a temporary commodity.[1] Scientific theories and models supply temporary explanations until better ones are discovered with more research, so science is never complete. Try to understand a variety of opinions, note them, and file them away for later if you are not sure how they fit together. If you are not ready to articulate an opinion, do not. If someone presses you, say "I have not formed my opinion yet because I am still learning." You might be surprised at the number of useless debates such honesty will spare you. Before you begin a journey to gain new knowledge, realize that you are entering a story already in progress. In time, you will form your own views and you may even alter the future course unfolding before you.

Having set the outlook, I offer these three steps for preparing to discuss science in the light of faith because they have served me well:

1. Know what the Church teaches.
2. Begin to learn the science.
3. Sort out the "system of wills."

FIND OUT WHAT THE CHURCH TEACHES

St. Thomas Aquinas, citing Aristotle, gave this reminder at the very beginning of his treatise *On Being and Essence*: "A small mistake in the beginning is a big one in the end."[2] The right first step is to allow yourself to experience awe and wonder when you see creation. See all of it as the handiwork of God, and know the teaching of your faith.

The Church's Magisterium was given the authority to define dogmas by Christ himself. According to the *Catechism of the Catholic Church*, Christians are obliged to an "irrevocable adherence of faith" to the truth contained in divine revelation (*CCC*, 88), but dogma is not an imposing boulder slammed down on its subjects, unyielding for all time. Church teaching is more like a light. As our understanding of God's revelation intensifies, the Magisterium makes light clearer and brighter for us by tending it—wiping away cloudiness, guarding the rays that have long illuminated the lives of Christians. The light remains what it is. Its keepers do not change the light to something else, but they help us to see the world and ourselves in the light of faith. The *Catechism* explains in the section titled "The dogmas of the faith":

> The Church's Magisterium exercises the authority it holds from Christ to the fullest extent when it defines dogmas, that is, when it proposes, in a form obliging the Christian people to an irrevocable adherence

of faith, truths contained in divine Revelation or also when it proposes, in a definitive way, truths having a necessary connection with these.

There is an organic connection between our spiritual life and the dogmas. Dogmas are lights along the path of faith; they illuminate it and make it secure. Conversely, if our life is upright, our intellect and heart will be open to welcome the light shed by the dogmas of faith.

The mutual connections between dogmas, and their coherence, can be found in the whole of the Revelation of the mystery of Christ. "In Catholic doctrine there exists an order or hierarchy of truths, since they vary in their relation to the foundation of the Christian faith." (*CCC*, 88–90)

Note that the words "dogma" and "doctrine" are both used. The word "doctrine" means teaching or instruction. Dogmas are doctrines, but they are more specific and directly connected to divine revelation whereas other teaching can derive from those truths but not be explicitly connected to them. For example, the doctrine of the Holy Trinity is a dogma because every articulation of that teaching is tied directly to what God revealed in scripture and tradition. (It is actually a rigorous theology course.) The teaching against contraception logically follows from divine revelation in that closing off openness to life and love in marital union contradicts the teaching of the Holy Trinity that we are made in the image and likeness of God to give and receive as completely as we can, creatively, but without becoming the other. That is why families are called reflections of the Holy Trinity, one body, many people. The "order of hierarchy of truths" refers to the logical flow. *Dogmas* are closest to revelation. Other *doctrines* radiate from them. Theological understanding can be further developed, and that is what is meant by the development of doctrine.

I think of the objectivity and development of understanding through a scientist mentality. There are dogmas in science, laws that

are observed directly in nature that are objective and cannot be denied
if conclusions drawn from them are to be correct. For example, if I do
not accept that the acceleration due to gravity on Earth is approxi-
mately 9.8 m/s^2 and instead pretend that 1.0 m/s^2 is the correct acceleration, and if my friend holds a book 100 meters above my head, and I
pretend I can stand there for 7.0 seconds without getting hit, all other
things being equal, then I get a knot on the head because I am wrong.

In both theology and physical science, new ways of communicating doctrines do not alter the truth; rather it means that our understanding has matured. Recall the meaning of "provisional" in science, a
word that refers to the temporary aspect of theories and models until
new data is gained. Doing scientific research requires us to reach into
the unknown world in which we live to discover more about it. Theology is different. Theology studies divine revelation, "unconditional"
truths given to us by God. We start with a deposit of truth that we
would not have found on our own; we grant assent and learn how
to articulate the articles of faith with human language. Revelation is
objectively true, like physical laws, in that our opinions of them do not
change them, and the discoveries of theology are related to our understanding of truth.

Theological understanding strives for better communication. For
example, the early Christians believed that bread and wine become the
Body and Blood of Christ, but the change was not called "transub-
stantiation" until St. Thomas Aquinas interpreted it according to the
categories of substance in Aristotelian philosophy.[3] Nothing new was
discovered, but a new way to express the same unconditional truth was
developed.

Even the way we think about dogmas and doctrine has changed. In
the first millennium of the Church, a theological opinion was declared
either heretical or orthodox. This history is summarized in nine-
teenth-century theologian Heinrich Denzinger's *Enchiridion Symbolorum: Compendium of Creeds, Definitions, and Declarations on Matters
of Faith and Morals.*[4] Beginning in the late Middle Ages, theological
qualifications to indicate the degree of certainty of doctrinal statements came into use. The distinctions theologians now use are more

nuanced and less black and white. A doctrine is "of divine faith" (*de fide divina*) if it is explicitly found in revelation.[5] These dogmas are of the highest certainty, directly revealed in scripture and confirmed by tradition, and address scripturally attested events such as creation, the fall, the Old and New Covenants, the Incarnation, and the Resurrection. A faithful Catholic may not deny them because to deny one of them would lead to a denial of more of them. A doctrine is "of divine and Catholic faith" (*de fide divina et catholica*) if it has also been formally defined for belief by the Church's Magisterium.[6] Propositions that are "close to the faith" (*fidei proxima*) are opinions that are held unanimously by the Church's theologians and regarded as revealed truth, but not defined as revealed.[7] But in addition to these high levels of certainty—and this is important—there are grades of theological opinion in the process of development that may be legitimately explored for furthering our understanding of truth.

The "hierarchy of truths" is important for navigating the questions. When you are sorting out challenging questions posed by scientific theory, it is of utmost importance that you clearly understand the difference between infallible dogmas and theological opinions that may legitimately be explored. Rejecting scientific conclusions that contradict dogmas is straightforward. We can never accept a conclusion that the soul does not exist or that God did not create the world with a beginning in time. Most of the interesting discussion lies in the areas where theological opinions are proposed and science can help deepen comprehension. How do we talk about the emergence and evolution of life? How do we describe the unity of body and soul? How do we think about the human person compared to other creatures? One of the most detrimental mistakes I have noticed in the debates is when a Catholic represents his or her theological or scientific opinion as certain dogma, although it has never been declared so by the Church. This behavior derails productive conversation and can damage souls.

There are a number of sources for researching the history of Church teaching. The *Catechism of the Catholic Church* is, of course, a good starting place. It is thoroughly referenced to specific encyclicals, councils, writings of the Church Fathers, and scripture. For detail on the historical development of dogma, Ludwig Ott's *Fundamentals of Catholic Dogma* and Heinrich Denzinger's *The Sources of Catholic Dogma* are trusted resources.[8] Ott's work identifies each dogma and labels its level of certainty, with a brief explanation about its development. Denzinger's volume is a chronologically arranged compendium of the councils and promulgations throughout the history of the Church.

A note to the wise: respect the real theologians and exegetes. All the faithful are encouraged to learn about the history of the Church and the development of dogma, but try not to play armchair theologian by promoting your new opinions as accepted teaching. It takes time and instruction to gain the skill necessary to understand how to identify the right questions and do the research to add new understanding to theology. Interpreting scripture requires training. If you are not a trained theologian who has committed to a course of study, do not appoint yourself an authority. Rather, find out who the legitimate authorities are, and read what they have written with the intent of learning and communicating their work.

BEGIN TO LEARN THE SCIENCE

I say "begin to learn" because new research is continually being reported and assimilated into existing theories. The hundreds of refereed journals published every month testify to the vitality of scientific inquiry. However, the deposit of science, so to speak, is not nearly as cogent and comprehensive as the history of dogmatic development. While the Magisterium of the Catholic Church guards the deposit of faith and keeps records of all developments—a magnificent treasure to the faithful—there is no single unifying magisterium of science that maintains, organizes, and vets the entire body of all scientific research. There are, however, textbooks, scholarly articles in refereed journals, conference proceedings, and all manner of books written.

So the best way to begin to learn about a field of science that interests you is to start reading. Read some popular science articles; they are good in that they usually provide a short summary and then reference a paper in a refereed journal. Pop science is also risky because the paper is interpreted by someone else. Look in textbooks or history books for concise summaries, and count reading a single chapter worthwhile. Textbooks are, to my mind, not given their proper appreciation. It takes years of work from groups of experts to pull a textbook together. They are arranged to teach. Textbooks can give you a good idea about how scientific theories become established over time. Studying the papers published by the Pontifical Academy of Sciences is a good way to stay up-to-date on the latest developments at the intersection of faith and science. When the academy hosts a working group on a specific topic, it publishes the short papers of the invited scholars.

Reading up on a particular subject is kind of like playing an adventure video game: you self-direct your path based on what you are interested in. Scientists speak in terms of layers of research. If you look up a reference from a magazine article, you are in the first layer. If you look up a reference in that reference because you want to know more about a certain point, you are in the second layer, and so on. You can chart a trail to new questions. This is how scientists break new ground—by plunging in, piecing together previous work, and figuring out what questions need to be addressed. I did it before attending graduate school and knew what I wanted to work on before I got there.

For instance, if you decide you want to learn more about quantum theory, you could start by reading the latest articles in a science digest. You could read just a few articles about string theory and follow references to the actual papers, which could lead you to read a single textbook chapter on the history of the discovery of subatomic particles, which could lead you to read the history of the development of quantum mechanics in general, which could spark an interest that has you browsing for updates to the research on a regular basis. You do not have to understand everything you read at once. Over time as you read more and more, it will start to fit together. You may even decide to become a scientist, especially if you find yourself designing experiments in your head to answer questions you notice are unanswered.

Again, a note for wisdom: respect the real scientists. I know some people bristle at that statement because so many scientists today are not people of faith, but if you have not conducted experiments, wrestled with the instrumentation, agonized over the data, discerned the analysis, and been ready to place your reputation behind the reporting of conclusions, it is hard to understand what it takes to add new knowledge to scientific disciplines. Reading a tidied-up summary in a journal is not the same thing as doing the work. Textbooks offer organized teachings on a subject, but they present knowledge sifted over much time, much hard work, and much failure between successes. The person who plays scientist after reading about science is like the person who thinks herself a cook after reading cookbooks.

But why, you might wonder, should one even care about science? Do we all have to love science? What if science is just not your thing? The answer is easy. We are all different, and we are not all made to love and appreciate the same things. Reflect on the words of St. Thérèse of Lisieux: "The science of love!" once exclaimed the Little Flower, "Ah! Sweet is the echo of that word to the ear of my soul! I desire no other science than that."[9] It is not necessary to know about the science of the physical world to know, love, and serve God like a saint.

Nevertheless, think of what modern science has done. For most of recorded history, religions provided the concepts and expressions for understanding nature, human life, and the cosmos. Since the emergence of a physical theory in the Christian Middle Ages, modern science has allowed us to quantify and describe the motions of smaller units of matter and more remote astronomical objects.

The modern person has a very different view of the world than people held before the rise of science. The quantum world seems nothing like the world we can see, yet we have every reason to conclude that those physical laws reasoned out by humans describe something true about reality. There is now evidence that the universe expanded from a singularity about 13.8 billion years ago. The possible events of its first few moments have been reconstructed in exceeding exactness. We now know that the Earth, once thought to be the center of the universe, is actually a seemingly insignificant speck orbiting the sun, which itself is a rather lost star in a spiral-shaped cluster of 200 billion stars rotating in space among thousands of galaxies existing within 100 million light-years of Earth. And the largest telescopes can detect billions of galaxies. In the time it took you to read that, the synapses in your brain probably fired hundreds of trillions of times while your body breathed in oxygen molecules that have traveled to your nose from God only knows where. All this knowledge greatly influences the way we think of our existence.

Theoretical physicists, even atheists, realize that when they interpret the messy world of observations and express their discoveries in the pristine world of mathematics, they are probing preexisting laws that govern the universe. Although the answer lies beyond science, scientists may consider where these preexisting laws came from. Unfortunately, even though universities append "doctor of philosophy" to their names, scientists do not generally gain much philosophical acumen through their education. They are not equipped to think about science in a greater context with the logical rigor good philosophy demands.

I still do not count myself an apt philosopher, but at least the word no longer induces a blank stare. I have learned that sound philosophy can stand on its own reasoning and sound theology can stand on its revelations. Science can at times deepen our understanding of philosophical or theological knowledge, but science should never be the foundation for that kind of knowledge. Science needs to be respected within its own legitimate limits. As St. Thérèse knew, and as I found out, science is less important than our bigger purpose of communion, love, and everlasting destiny.

SORT OUT THE SYSTEM OF WILLS

These first two steps will not always be completed in blocks. Often a scientific question will spur a question about what the Church teaches and vice versa. When it is time to bring together what you know about what the Church teaches and what you have learned about science, and you find that some points seem to contradict each other or present problems, think of faith as shining a light onto the question to guide the way. There is no harm in learning what scientists find if you know your faith. You do not have to agree with everything you read. As you start to form opinions, learn how to qualify them as such and be careful not to overstate your position. Do not—and I cannot stress this enough—be sensationalistic. Do not conjure up speculations for attention. You will confuse people. Seek to explain and illuminate because the faith-and-science dialogue needs communicators.

Most of your work should be to understand the work of scientists and theologians. Do not try to find some insight about how science proves an aspect of faith because that is not the role of science. In my opinion, the dialogue is about more than reconciliation; it is about elevation. We are not trying to fit faith into science or vice versa, nor are we only trying to restore unity. The dialogue is ultimately meant to raise human insight, like wings raise an eagle. The often-quoted remark from St. John Paul II to the (then) Director of the Vatican Observatory, Rev. George V. Coye, S.J., in a June 1, 1988, letter states the twofold nature of the dialogue. "Science can purify religion from error and superstition; religion can purify science from idolatry and false absolutes. Each can draw the other into a wider world, a world in which both can flourish."[10]

It is time to talk about this wider world. I have termed it the "system of wills" for the sake of communicating how to understand the physical and biological sciences in the scope of other disciplines, but the system is based upon St. Thomas Aquinas's teaching. He explained in the *Summa Theologiæ* that there is an order in nature of causes and effects.[11] God is the first cause, the Creator, so he is not subject to secondary causes, such as change and motion in the physical realm. God created everything and holds all things visible and invisible in existence. In the Nicene Creed the word "invisible" refers to the spiritual (immaterial) realm, but there is another invisible realm as well, that of the atom. God holds the particles that are invisible to the human eye but material nonetheless in existence too, as they move around according to the created laws that govern them.

As St. Thomas asserts citing St. Augustine, God's law is the "supreme law."[12] Everything created, in entirety, is subject to this supreme law. The physical realm of matter follows the laws of nature created by God. The realm of beings with wills, angels, humans, and animals are movers in the physical realm. If there were no other created being with any kind of will and intellect, then the material realm would follow, to the elementary units of matter and energy, the laws of physics as God designed and determined them. The only will that could alter the particles following laws of physics would be God's will. Thus, the will is a mover.

Before any created being is inserted into the system of wills, a point needs to be stated. *This purity of physical system is how a physical scientist calculates.* It is no different when a baker tries to figure out how much butter to put in a pastry recipe. A chemist or a physicist works by defining an isolated system to the best of his or her ability, removing every other factor, controlling the variables, and examining the effects of changing other variables. The scientist is aware that the system exists in the surrounding of the rest of the universe that contains beings and that the universe is not absolutely closed and inanimate. The scientist is self-aware of the experimentation underway by the use of his own free will and intellect. Nevertheless, *there is no mathematical accounting for free will in the isolated systems of chemistry or physics.* We will return to this point in the chapter about quantum mechanics and free will.

For now, the purpose is to emphasize the point. The isolation of physical systems needs to be appreciated in the faith-and-science dialogue. For physical scientists trained to think this acutely, the mechanical mindset is hard to escape. Remember this when you consider the theories of scientists. They speak in terms of isolated systems physical systems.

Now let us consider the larger system that includes created beings. The rational beings with free will and intellect are the angels (bodiless souls) and humans (body and soul). Just as God can will to move particles, so too can rational beings created with free will, but in limited ways, the ways which God designed them. We can kick rocks, overcome grumpiness if we are hungry, and build integrated circuits capable of storing entire libraries; we cannot change a rock into diamond, live indefinitely without food, or make children stop growing.

It helps to compare humans and angels briefly, although our focus in this consideration of faith and science will remain on humans since we are the ones who do science. In his treatise on the angels in the *Summa Theologiæ*, St. Thomas Aquinas, referencing Pseudo-Dionysius, a theologian and philosopher from the late fifth to early sixth century, says that angels are purely intellectual beings or "heavenly minds."[13] Their dignity surpasses that of humans. Intellect for angels is perfect at once "from their very nature" in that they instantly know all they are created to know.[14] Angels very well may know, if God wills it, all about the location of electrons in any atom. As free agents, angels can intervene in an otherwise strictly physical reality too. Since the angels who chose goodness, apprehend only goodness, they always will what is good.[15] The angels who chose evil always choose evil. Indeed one may rightly wonder about the unrealized benefits guardian angels can be to scientists, but I digress.

The point is: we have a lower intellect than the angels. Aquinas explains that humans pursue perfection in knowledge of truth by "discursive intellectual operation."[16] Humans must advance from one thing to another rationally, as we do using the scientific method, wherein we observe, hypothesize, experiment, and form conclusions and new questions for the next round. "Discursive" implies progressing in a slow or irregular manner, sometimes over a wide range of topics. For angels, there is no discursive process because "in the truths which they know naturally, they at once behold all things whatsoever that can be known in them."[17] Likewise, our choices to act cause us to intervene in an otherwise deterministic world to move matter, just as angels can and just as God does.

Do these matter movers with free will break the laws of physics? St. Thomas says, "Therefore since the order of nature is given to things by God, if He does anything outside this order, it is not against nature."[18] In the hypothetical case that only God and physical creation existed, God's intervention to move particles outside the created order would not be called a miracle because if God wills to move particles, nothing has happened outside the supreme law. The word "miracle" refers to our admiration for a manifest effect whose cause is hidden outside the order in which we (humans) know.[19] That is to say: without humans in the system of wills, there are no miracles.

To tie all of this together, I borrow a concept from the great thinker, C. S. Lewis. In his 1947 book *Miracles*, he refers to nature as a "hostess." I also like his use of the word "incommoded." Of the intervention in physical nature he says, "We see every day that physical nature is not in the least incommoded by the daily inrush of events from biological nature or from psychological nature."[20] If a cup of tea is invaded with sugar, for example, physical laws rush to accommodate the newcomer. If tea is stirred, physical laws follow suit.

In perhaps a less elegant manner owed to years of materialist thinking, I prefer to think of nature as a "medium" rather than a pleasantly smiling female eager to fetch the cookies. Matter and energy follow laws of physics, designed by God, and they form the *physical medium* in which we live, a medium that accommodates the actions of our free will. Therefore, when a violinist pulls her bow across the strings to make music, she intervenes and nature accommodates. If we throw a ball off the roof, it falls to the ground and, unless another person intercepts it, the projectile motion is calculable. To repeat, these actions of free agents are not breaking the laws of nature—they are following the laws of both nature and supernature, the total system.

Consistent with St. Thomas Aquinas, Lewis also emphasizes that miracles do not break the laws of nature, for they are factors that affect nature that are beyond nature. We see it at every Mass. The bread and wine become the Body and Blood of Christ, miraculously. We receive it into our bodies, and our digestive system digests it. If a woman becomes pregnant, the physical medium surrounding the child accommodates his or her conception. *The supreme law and laws of nature are interlocked.* If a man builds a house and a couple raises a family, they surely have altered the course of uncountable atoms, even if most of them are far away and affected by an infinitesimal amount. Nature *assimilates* our actions, harmonizing them with physical events.[21] If we throw parties, build homes, mend clothes, decorate windows, or change the oil in automobiles, we intervene in nature. You get the point: our activity causes matter to change, extensively, and beyond what matter left to its own devices would accomplish. As nature's particles accommodate the interventions of free agents, they do so by following preordained laws of physics and chemistry. We do not change the laws. Nature accommodates us. We are higher in the order of causes and effects than the horsehair and wood that constitutes violin bows.

God created physical matter and God created free agents, so together these form the whole systematic universe. The laws of physics may cover the whole of time and space, but as Lewis puts it, "what they leave out is precisely the whole real universe—the incessant torrent of actual events which makes up true history."[22]

Lewis goes on to say that a "miracle is emphatically not an event without cause or without results" either.[23] Christianity obliges us to acknowledge that God can intervene in the world for the sake of our salvation by causing miracles. What is a miracle, then? St. Thomas calls a miracle something God does outside the order of nature "which we know."[24] To us, it may seem like breaking laws of physics, but miracles do not break the supreme law. In addition, if God wills to move particles, it cannot be modeled or predicted with human calculation, and that is why physics cannot study miracles.

Does this mean that in the past humans have mistaken events for miracles when, in fact, they simply did not yet understand the physics? Perhaps, but God would have known the extent of human understanding at that time. Does this mean that angels can move matter, but we can mistake the event for a miracle? Perhaps, but the good angels only will what is good. Does this mean that, in theory, if we could stop time and motion and study all particles fully, we would find all the physical laws? Perhaps, but I have no expectation of ever achieving that, although it is an enjoyable thought. Does this mean there might be a hierarchy of wills, and those higher animals such as dogs fit into this hierarchy (much higher than cats) and can therefore intervene in nature and be accommodated by it? Yes, I think so. There are no physics equations that could account for my German shepherd's behavior when she sees the first robin in April. All speculation aside, we can say with certainty that mathematical models will never fully account for every particle's motion because of the free will of rational beings.

Thinking in terms of this system of wills has helped me to sort out *every* faith and science question, and that is why I have explained it and will elaborate on it throughout the book.

PART II

QUESTIONS IN THE PHYSICAL SCIENCES

CHAPTER 4

DOES THE BIG BANG PROVE GOD?

A STORY STILL BEING WRITTEN

In 1927, Belgian abbé and physicist Msgr. Georges Lemaître published in a Belgian astronomy journal a paper showing he had solved Albert Einstein's equations of general relativity to yield a model of the universe that could be traced back in time to an originating single point. In 1931, Fr. Lemaître republished this work in English in the *Monthly Notices of the Royal Astronomical Society*: "Expansion of the Universe: "A Homogeneous Universe of Constant Mass and Increasing Radius Accounting for the Radial Velocity of Extra-galactic Nebulae."[1] Fr. Lemaître's solution of Einstein's gravitational field equations described an expanding universe in contrast to the variable radius, uniform density universe postulated by Einstein and the zero-density, empty universe postulated by Willem de Sitter.

Also in 1931, Fr. Lemaître published a letter, titled "The Beginning of the World from the Point of View of Quantum Theory," that hypothesized a "primeval atom."[2] Here is how he described it: "At the origin, all the mass of the universe would exist in the form of a unique atom; the radius of the universe, although not strictly zero, being relatively small. The whole universe would be produced by the disintegration of this primeval atom." Fred Hoyle later labeled this event the Big Bang.

Two decades later, and as support for the theory grew, Pope Pius XII made a logical inference in an address to the 1951 Plenary

Session of the Pontifical Academy of Sciences titled "The Proofs for
the Existence of God in the Light of Modern Natural Science." The
pope enthusiastically argued that the Big Bang was scientific evidence
for creation—that science had become a witness to that "primordial
Fiat Lux, uttered at the moment when, along with matter, there burst
forth from nothing a sea of light and radiation, while the particles of
chemical elements split and formed into millions of galaxies."[3] The
pope suggested that the Big Bang theory was scientific evidence for
God. "Hence, creation took place in time. Therefore, there is a Creator.
Therefore, God exists! Although it is neither explicit nor complete,
this is the reply we were awaiting from science, and which the present
human generation is awaiting from it."[4]

As the story goes, Fr. Lemaître intervened after this address to
the Pontifical Academy of Sciences. He was a high-ranking member of the academy and contacted the science advisor to the pope. Fr.
Lemaître was not in favor of such strong statements because he knew
that his theory was subject to further revision. He insisted that the
developing scientific theories be judged on their scientific merits alone
and not be used in support of theological conclusions.[5]

Fr. Lemaître's counsel must have been convincing. Less than a year
later, the pope addressed 650 astronomers in Rome for the Eighth
General Assembly of the International Astronomical Union. This
address praised the scientists for their work, but there was no mention of how the Big Bang provides evidence or proof of the Creator.[6]
According to George Coyne, former director of the Vatican Observatory who wrote an essay on the issue, "Never again did Pius XII attribute any philosophical, metaphysical, or religious implications to the
theory of the Big Bang."[7]

The pope was clear, however, in his address to the 1951 Plenary
Session of the Pontifical Academy of Sciences that science, as I have
highlighted already, is continually developing and that absolute proof
of creation is outside the limits of science. This is what the pope had
said immediately following the *Fiat Lux* statement:

It is quite true that the facts established up to the present time are not an absolute proof of creation in time, as are the proofs drawn from metaphysics and Revelation in what concerns simple creation or those founded on Revelation if there be question of creation in time. The pertinent facts of the natural sciences, to which We have referred, are awaiting still further research and confirmation, and the theories founded on them are in need of further development and proof before they can provide a sure foundation for arguments which, of themselves, are outside the proper sphere of the natural sciences.[8]

Fr. Lemaître surely knew his theory would be argued, amended, or expanded as more accurate mathematics, observations, and explanations were obtained, and he advised great caution against using science to prove what we hold in faith. Today the Big Bang theory is the predominant cosmological model for the earliest moments of the universe, defended by religious believers and nonbelievers alike. Yet after almost ninety years the theory remains a theory in continual development.

Fast-forward this story to March 2014. The journal *Nature* reported that astronomers had detected the first evidence of primordial gravitational waves from 13.8 billion years ago with the BICEP2 telescope at the South Pole. This detection was heralded online at *Nature Breaking News* with the following statement: "Astronomers have peered back to nearly the dawn of time and found what seems to be the long-sought 'smoking gun' for the theory that the Universe underwent a spurt of wrenching, exponential growth called inflation during the first tiny fraction of a second of its existence."[9] There was much excitement because the detection of these waves had been predicted as proof of the cosmic inflation that followed the Big Bang.

Shortly thereafter, *CNN Belief Blog* ran an article titled "Does the Big Bang Breakthrough Offer Proof of God?"[10] The article was written by Dr. Leslie Wickman, a former Lockheed Martin corporate astronaut, rocket scientist, and engineer on NASA's Hubble Space Telescope and International Space Station programs. Affirming biblical beliefs in the light of this new scientific report, she wrote, "So this latest discovery is good news for us believers, as it adds scientific support to the idea that the universe was caused—or created—by something or someone outside it and not dependent on it." In her subsequent book *God of the Big Bang: How Modern Science Affirms the Creator*, Wickman wrote that the CNN article went viral with over half a million views in less than a week, ranking in the top five of the world's most shared news stories on social media, presumably in that week.[11]

By September 2014, however, doubt had been cast on the reliability of the "smoking gun." Another group of researchers at the European Space Agency's Planck space observatory compiled a map of interstellar dust that substantially lowered the chances that the South Pole telescope had found the gravitational waves from the dawn of time. In January 2015, *Nature* ran a story titled "Gravitational Waves Discovery Now Officially Dead."[12] As it turned out, what astronomers had thought to be gravitational waves of cosmic origin was actually Milky Way dust. The excitement over the "smoking gun" had been premature, but such is the way of the scientific method.

In 2016, physicists at the Laser Interferometer Gravitational-Wave Observatory (LIGO) in Hanford, Washington and Livingston, Louisiana again reported that they had detected the gravitational waves, as *Science Magazine* reported it, "fulfilling a 4-decade quest and opening new eyes on the heavens."[13] Physicists think the observed waves were produced when two black holes, about 29 and 36 times the mass of the sun, merged 1.3 billion years ago.[14] These waves provide information about the origin of gravity. This significant discovery is a milestone, but even more, it is expected to be the beginning of new astronomical discoveries.[15]

Throughout this story, there is an overarching question about what kind of proof science can offer to faith. Some scholars, such as Fr. Lemaître, warn against using scientific theories in support of theological conclusions. Other scholars, such as Pope Pius XII and Dr. Wickman, did say that science can affirm a Creator. At this moment in history, the Big Bang is a more certain theory than ever before because the gravitational waves have been confirmed, so it seems appropriate to call the Big Bang an "affirmation" of the existence of God. Nonetheless, Fr. Lemaître's admonishment still seems appropriate. As this story shows, we do not know what scientists will report next, and we do not know how our affirmations will be perceived.

How many of the half a million people around the world who read Dr. Wickman's article were confused when the evidence for God was declared dead? Or worse, how many people now think science has vindicated God's existence since the waves were observed at LIGO?

The lesson is that both writers and readers need to heed the language. Both Pope Pius XII and Dr. Wickman were careful to cite Big Bang discoveries as *inductive* evidence (affirmation) to accompany other *deductive* evidence, but these distinctions seem to be hidden in the discussion. I think they are key. Therefore, before you decide to what extent science can provide proof of faith, a discussion of the difference between inductive and deductive reasoning is warranted.

INDUCTIVE AND DEDUCTIVE PROOFS

Inductive proofs widen from details to a broad, but only probable, conclusion. They reason from particulars, such as those details of the Big Bang discoveries, to generals, such as the existence of God as the First Cause or Intelligent Designer. Deductive proofs narrow from broad statements (premises) to absolute conclusions. For example, one may argue that past time is either finite or infinite. If it can be shown with reason that it is highly unlikely for time to be infinite, then by default, it is highly likely that time is finite. In general, scientific proofs are inductive and theological proofs are deductive, although both science and theology can rely on both types of proofs or combinations of them. For our purposes, let us clarify the difference in the two types.

Here is an example of the difference between inductive and deductive proofs. Using inductive reasoning, my children might call the particular facts that I feed them dinner every night, wash their laundry routinely, and put bandages on their boo boos when they bleed evidence or proof of the bigger principle that I love them. With enough evidence over time from routine provision, substantiated by my verbal affirmations of fondness for them, my children could reasonably conclude that my actions are indeed proof of my love. This is an inductive proof. The facts complement (complete or go well with) each other and corroborate (affirm, confirm, or give support to) the larger conclusion, but, alas, they cannot absolutely prove the claim.

Objectively speaking, the fact that I feed them, clean up after them, and care for them does not lead, with certainty, to the sole conclusion that I love them. The rapscallions could call my dutiful, consistent nourishment and nurturing "evidence" that I love them in the sense that it is factual grounds for belief in the highly probable conclusion that I do love them. But they could also argue that I am only pretending to love them and that I have other motives deep in my heart. They could argue that they do not have all the information. They could decide that I actually resent them and cook, clean, and apply gauzes just to keep them quiet. They could search for facts to prove that conclusion instead. They could grow up, and after all I did for them, they could still say, "Nope, I am just not convinced Mom loves us."

A deductive proof might involve one of them arguing that I either love them or I do not—that one or the other conclusion has to be true. If they can reason that there is no other scenario in which I would care for them as I do because I do it so well and I do it with purpose, that no one is forcing me to do it, that I have no other possible ulterior motive to do it, that my motherly actions have to be explained by love and only love, then they can deduce the conclusion that I love them. Here is the zinger. As anyone knows who has articulated the most elegant of arguments, even deductive proofs can fail to convince a person.

That example shows the human dimension of proofs. We are free agents in the system of wills (see chapter 3) looking at the created world around us and trying to figure it out. Both inductive and deductive proofs will not convince a person unless a person is willing to accept the conclusion. Inductive proofs may seem weaker because they only point to probable conclusions. Deductive proofs may seem stronger because they demand a conclusion with probative force. Nevertheless, proofs are like glasses of water. You can purify that water and set it down in all the fine crystal you want, but you cannot force a person to drink it in.

Let us now consider two different views from two more Catholic scientists on the extent to which scientific theories should contribute to the understanding of Christian doctrine.

The first view holds that a theory accepted by a consensus of scientists can deepen the understanding of faith. In this view, theologians and philosophers should combine accepted scientific claims with metaphysical premises to discover new insights; since the Big Bang theory is widely accepted and since it provides physical evidence of a high probability of a beginning in time, the Big Bang is cited as evidence of creation and of God's existence. In this view, modern science complements and corroborates metaphysical arguments as strong inductive proof.

For example, Fr. Robert J. Spitzer, S.J., physicist, philosopher, educator, author, and founder and currently active president of the Magis Center of Reason and Faith, argues the following early on in his 2010 book *New Proofs for the Existence of God: Contributions of Contemporary Physics and Philosophy*: "Even though scientific conclusions are subject to change in the light of new data, we should not let this possibility cause us to unnecessarily discount the validity of long-standing, persistent, rigorously established theories. If we did this, we might discount the majority of our scientific theories. Thus, it is reasonable and responsible to attribute qualified truth value to such theories until such time as new data requires them to be changed."[16]

The book begins with an in-depth review of current developments in cosmology, particularly the Borde-Guth-Vilenkin theorem. This theorem states that inflationary-model universes must have a beginning of past time, which implies a creation event. However, Fr. Spitzer is clear that the theorem is used as inductive proof. He explains that the wide agreement among scientists that the universe has a finite beginning in time gives credence to classical and medieval arguments for the existence of God. Confidence in the philosophical ideas about God's existence has been lost in the modern era, and the new proofs Fr. Spitzer lays out in his book are meant to restore that confidence.

Fr. Spitzer reformulates philosophical and metaphysical proofs for the existence of an unconditioned reality and a Creator of past time.[17] These metaphysical proofs are deductive; that is, they are reasoned from general principles down to final conclusions with probative force. Thus, the proofs from cosmology are inductive evidence that fits with the stronger deductive proofs. As Fr. Spitzer articulates very clearly in his book, just as Pope Pius XII did, the scientific theories cannot by themselves prove or disprove God's existence, but they can add to the appreciation of it.

A second Catholic view on the influence of science on our understanding of Christian doctrine was defended by Dr. Peter Hodgson, a particle physicist and fellow of Corpus Christi College at Oxford University, where he headed the Nuclear Physics Theoretical Group. In his 2005 book *Theology and Modern Physics*, Dr. Hodgson explains that the provisional nature of science "sets severe limits on, or even excludes" drawing any theological conclusions from it. Here is how Hodgson puts it:

> By experiments in the laboratory we attain some knowledge of the laws of nature, and then we extend them to the realms of the very small and the very large, and to the distant past. Sometimes they break down, as they did for the atom and at very high velocities, and this led to quantum mechanics and special relativity. How then can we be sure that our present understanding is adequate to discuss what happened billions of years ago? Very small changes in the laws, quite undetectable by us, could have large effects when applied to the whole universe. Yet in spite of this difficulty, we must extrapolate the laws of nature, because we have no alternative, but it is important to remember the provisional character of all our knowledge of the distant past, as this sets severe limits on, or even excludes, any possibility of drawing theological conclusions.[18]

Dr. Hodgson is more focused on the fact that scientific models have limits. Quantum theory showed us that the classical laws of mechanics, for example, do not adequately describe the motion of subatomic particles. The Big Bang theory applies the laws of physics for subatomic particles as they are known at present to the earliest moments of the universe. As widely accepted as the theory may be, there are still discoveries to be made, and he is sensitive to this ever-unfolding aspect of science.

Do you think science can provide strong inductive proof of the tenets of faith? How careful should the language about proofs be? Or do you think the provisional nature of science prohibits the possibility of drawing theological or metaphysical conclusions from science?

I will explain my opinion. I am inclined to agree with the perspective of Dr. Hodgson that severe limits should be put on drawing theological insights from science. As a scientist, when philosophers or theologians get too excited about science, I find myself thinking, "Leave the science alone, and do not try to make science do more than it can do!" You will not see me cite any single scientific discovery or prediction as proof of God's existence, not even inductively, because I do not know what will be discovered tomorrow or next year. I do not want to give the impression that science demonstrates the existence of God because I already believe God exists before I ever get to science.

In my view, seeing science as evidence of God is an *all-or-none proposition*. I see the atom—everything that makes it up and everything made from atomic particles yet discovered—as evidence of the Creator, but only in the same way I see a dandelion or a sunset as proof of God.

On the other hand, I have learned what philosophy and metaphysics seek to do, and I have come to appreciate Fr. Spitzer's approach as well. While his volume is generally received as a modern expression of the classical proofs of God's existence, I see it as valuable in a different way. He shows how *sound reasoning ought to lead scientific questioning*. Fr. Spitzer's book offers the kind of guidance a scientist not trained in philosophy needs. If a scientist understood from the outset what conclusions were metaphysically unlikely, then the scientist would have more tools to make research decisions. The right answer to the wrong question is not much use.

Stepping back, I want to say something more basic about what the Church teaches. Whether physics in our lifetime points to a beginning of the universe or not, Catholics still affirm a beginning because we hold that truth in faith. Before the Big Bang theory, when people thought the universe and time are infinite, the Church held to her creed. This belief is ancient, forming an unbroken thread all the way back to Genesis. The Old Testament people held a belief in creation in time. The early Christians defended that belief against the pantheistic ideas of ancient Greek philosophy. And today, we need to be absolutely clear about the limits of science; if scientists include the assumption of infinite time in their theories now or in the future (and some do), it should not shake our faith. St. Thomas Aquinas expressed that the rejection of the eternity of the world was a matter of faith in divine revelation and *not* a matter of scientific demonstration or reason: "The articles of faith cannot be proved demonstratively, because *faith is of things that appear not* (Heb 11:1). But that God is the Creator of the world: hence that the world began is an article of faith; for we say, I believe in one God."[19]

Physical and biological sciences are limited to questions about the material realm. Metaphysics, philosophy, and theology are separate disciplines with their own methods. They deal with meaning, purpose, and destiny and are broader endeavors than physical or biological science.

We will wrap up this discussion with the instruction from the International Theological Commission published in 2004, "Communion and Stewardship: Human Persons Created in the Image of God." This text states the following regarding Big Bang cosmology and faith: "With respect to the *creatio ex nihilo* [creation out of nothing], theologians can note that the Big Bang theory does not contradict this doctrine insofar as it can be said that the supposition of an absolute beginning is not scientifically inadmissible. Since the Big Bang theory does not in fact exclude the possibility of an antecedent stage of matter, it can be noted that the theory appears to provide merely *indirect* support for the doctrine of *creatio ex nihilo* which as such can only be known by faith."[20]

Note that the commission says the Big Bang theory provides only *"indirect* support" (the italics are theirs) for the doctrine of creation out of nothing and note that the language is cautious as in the use of the phrases "not scientifically inadmissible" and "does not in fact exclude."

In my view, if we see all of science as the study of the handiwork of God, then all of it—as it is known and as it emerges—is evidence of the Creator. This view prevents the need to single out any scientific discoveries, but it also allows us to express awe and wonder.

ALL-OR-NONE PROPOSITION

One has but to browse the history of science to know that once firmly held ideas are frequently (on the scale of decades) overturned by new ones. Aristotle thought the Earth was fixed. Louis Pasteur demonstrated that microorganisms do not spontaneously generate from air. Mendeleev once calculated the atomic weight of the ether, and Lord Kelvin thought atoms were vortexes in that medium. Thomson thought electrons were corpuscles—negatively charged particles surrounded by a soup of positive charge, like raisins in pudding. Bohr's model of the hydrogen atom did not explain why negatively charged electrons did not collapse into the positively charged nucleus. In 2015, physicists confirmed evidence of the pentaquark, a subatomic particle made up of five quarks that is predicted to provide further information about how stars form.

There is nothing wrong with seeing nature as evidence of God. Nothing is flawed about that view at all, and it is perfectly consistent with Genesis and with what believers profess in the Apostles' Creed: "I believe in God, the Father Almighty, Creator of heaven and earth."

What I want to stress is that this worldview is an all-or-none proposition. A believer views creation as the handiwork of God, all of it in consistently interacting totality, as an act of faith. We start there, just as we start there when we bless our meals. It makes no sense to view some findings of science as evidence for God and some findings as random information unworthy of much appreciation. For

the logophiles (word lovers) out there, it is the difference in ubiquitous (omnipresent) and nullibiquitous (existing nowhere).[21] If the Big
Bang is evidence of God, then so are the electron and the pentaquark;
so is the biological machinery of photosynthesis; so is the seed; so
is the *Ginkgo biloba* tree; so is the forest; so are all the cliffs, rocks,
and grains of soil; so is every carbon, hydrogen, oxygen, and nitrogen
atom in every side chain specific to every amino acid; so is DNA; so
is a living cell; so is the starlight that traveled for years to reach the
Earth; so are the eyes that sense the light and the brain that processes
the input; so are the bacteria in guts; and so are the mosquitoes with
their creepy tubelike mouthparts that pierce skin and suck blood. We
are compelled by faith to believe this. "For the invisible things of him,
from the creation of the world, are clearly seen, being understood by
the things that are made; his eternal power also, and divinity: so that
they are inexcusable" (Rom 1:20).

The belief that in the beginning God created the universe is a
starting point for the study of creation. Naming the Big Bang as evidence for a Creator makes sense as an expression of the kind of wonder a child feels when he marvels at trees, clouds, bugs, or the Big
Dipper—the kind of wonder any of us feels in looking at the natural
world around us. As St. Thomas makes clear, "it necessarily follows
that all things, inasmuch as they participate in existence, must likewise be subject to divine providence."[22] The universe is intelligently
designed, and we believe so in faith.

THE BIBLE, CHRISTIANITY, AND COSMOLOGY

The work of the late Fr. Stanley L. Jaki helped me to understand science in the context of the Catholic faith. Jaki was a priest, a theologian, a physicist, a historian, and a philosopher; he therefore possessed
a vast store of knowledge that gave him a breadth of insight. He did
not study history, for instance, as an isolated timeline, but rather in the
context of theology, culture, technology, literature, and artwork so that
he could find the origins of certain cultural psychologies that affected
the behaviors of people. He was awarded the 1987 Templeton Prize

"for being a leading thinker in areas at the boundary of science and theology."[23]

Suffice it to say that physical science *did* emerge in a Christian culture for a reason.[24] Fr. Jaki demonstrated with exhaustive historical research in his 1974 volume *Science and Creation: From Eternal Cycles to an Oscillating Universe* that science was born of Christianity because of this teaching that there is a beginning and an end in time and that the universe is created with order.[25] The case can be made by contrasting the religious and cosmological views of ancient cultures with Christianity. Other cultures held a fundamentally pantheistic or animistic mythological view of an eternally cycling universe.[26] Scientific enterprise thrived to a limited extent in ancient Egypt, Mesopotamia, pre-Columbian America, China, India, Babylon, Greece, and Arabia; but the science of physical laws and systems of laws to describe the cosmos never emerged as a universal discipline the way it did in Christian culture. The cultures contributed scientific talent and ingenuity to the ability to manipulate matter, but they did not seek to articulate the nature of matter in terms of first principles (primary propositions which further reasoning is based upon) derived from experimentation.

The Egyptians pictured parts of the world as animal gods. The goal of Taoism for the Chinese was to merge into the rhythm of cosmic cycles. Confucius taught that the individual should seek what is in himself and leave external things to their natural destiny. The Hindus held the doctrine of the atman, the Indian expression for "first principle," which taught that the individual self should strive to lay hold of the ultimate Soul of the Universe, the Atman, who bred himself. His mouth, nostrils, eyes, and ears became distinct of his own doing. His skin and hair became the plants and trees, and his heart the moon. His semen became water and his navel exuded corruption.[27] This world-soul is understood as an endless cycle of births and decays with no starting or ending points. Fr. Jaki compares it to an eternal "cosmic treadmill."[28]

For the Babylonians, the *Enuma Elish* was a portrayal of personified forces engaged in bloody battles. They thought that the mother goddess, Tiamat, was dismembered to form the sky, earth, water, and air. Such cosmogonies, or accounts of the generation of the universe, did not place significance on physical first principles or on a systematic investigation of elemental particles. All of these ancient cultures believed in an eternally cycling cosmos.

The radically different concept of a Creator and creation out of nothing was literally codified in the ancient Hebrew culture. Usually the Hebrew culture of the Old Testament is not considered in the history of science, but Fr. Jaki notes a most important contribution from them because of their faithfulness to the concept of a Creator and creation out of nothing. If science can be said to have been "born" in the Christian Middle Ages, then the ancient Hebrew culture was the nurturing womb that allowed science to emerge as a viable discipline in the medieval universities.

The following is a very brief review of scripture from the Old Testament and writings from the early Church Fathers. There are many more verses and quotes to include, and Fr. Jaki does in his much longer book, but these are offered to at least demonstrate the point. The understanding of creation was necessary, which is to say, the biblical worldview was necessary for the birth of modern science.

When the Israelites in Babylonian captivity hoped for the restoration of Jerusalem, the word of the Lord came to Jeremiah to remind the people that it is God who orders the day and night and God who promised heirs to David's throne with descendants as countless as the "stars of the heaven" and measureless as the "sand of the sea"(Jer 33:22). The nations were told to submit to God's will and obey his commands.

God's unchallenged power is often mentioned in Isaiah. "Who hath measured the waters in the hollow of his hand, and weighed the heavens with his palm? Who hath poised with three fingers the bulk of the earth, and weighed the mountains in scales, and the hills in a balance?"(Is 40:12). Isaiah points to the order and measure of physical objects as contributing proof of God's omniscience (having all knowledge). The Israelites knew they had to trust the faithfulness of God because they knew that humans are not the ones who order the day and the night. They believed that the law of God extended to all things moral, societal, and natural, including the order and measure of physical objects and motion.

The first three chapters of Proverbs contain three series of instructions about wise behavior; the starting point is a reference to God's wisdom in the created world, its stability of creation and the firmness of the heavens and the earth. The praise of wisdom goes on for five more chapters and ends with a personification of God's wisdom. When you read this passage, think of the scientific significance of the "I" that is God's wisdom of creation and the "children of men" who would be scientists:

> The Lord possessed me in the beginning of his ways, before he made any thing from the beginning. I was set up from eternity, and of old before the earth was made. The depths were not as yet, and I was already conceived, neither had the fountains of waters as yet sprung out: The mountains with their huge bulk had not as yet been established: before the hills I was brought forth: He had not yet made the earth, nor the rivers, nor the poles of the world.
>
> When he prepared the heavens, I was present: when with a certain law and compass he enclosed the depths: When he established the sky above, and poised the fountains of waters: When he compassed the sea with its bounds, and set a law to the waters that they should not pass their limits: when he balanced the foundations of the earth; I was with him forming all things: and was delighted every day, playing before him at all time; Playing in the world: and my delights were to be with the children of men. Now therefore, ye children, hear me: Blessed are they that keep my ways. (Prv 8:22–32)

The Old Testament is the story of the unity of cosmic and human history. The Book of Wisdom shows an appreciation for Hellenistic

Greek culture, but through the lens of belief in a Creator of the universe and source of all wisdom who "ordered all things in measure, and number, and weight" (Ws 11:21). The Book of Wisdom was written in Alexandria around the first century BC, as Jewish thinkers came into contact with Hellenistic learning in Alexandria. There was a cultural refinement between the polytheistic nature worship of the Greeks and the creation *ex nihilo* in the unique worldview of the people of the Covenant. The author of the Book of Wisdom appreciates the knowledge of the Hellenistic culture.

> For he hath given me the true knowledge of the things that are: to know the disposition of the whole world, and the virtues of the elements, The beginning, and ending, and midst of the times, the alterations of their courses, and the changes of seasons, The revolutions of the year, and the dispositions of the stars, The natures of living creatures, and rage of wild beasts, the force of winds, and reasonings of men, the diversities of plants, and the virtues of roots, And all such things as are hid and not foreseen, I have learned: for wisdom, which is the worker of all things, taught me. (Ws 7:17–21)

The Hellenistic Jews held a sacred respect for the books of the Maccabees, which contain the first biblical reference to creation *ex nihilo* in the story about the mother who was martyred after witnessing the torture and martyrdom of her seven sons in the second book. That mother shows us definitively how to view everything in the light of faith.

She and her sons are tortured not for any crime but for refusing to break God's command not to eat the flesh of swine. The mother watches as her sons are tortured one by one—their tongues cut out, their scalps torn off, their hands and feet mutilated—while she and the remaining brothers stand by. She watches as each son is roasted alive, maimed and suffering, and she does not panic. She acts the way Holy

Mother Mary acted in front of the Cross, witnessing another seemingly senseless death of a son. The brothers encourage each other as they die bravely. They say, "The Lord God will look upon the truth, and will take pleasure in us" (2 Mc 7:6). As they die, the mother continues to speak to her sons, "joining a man's heart to a woman's thought": "I know not how you were formed in my womb: for I neither gave you breath, nor soul, nor life, neither did I frame the limbs of every one of you. But the Creator of the world, that formed the nativity of man, and that found out the origin of all, he will restore to you again in his mercy, both breath and life, as now you despise yourselves for the sake of his laws" (2 Mc 7:21–23).

Outraged at this defiance of his authority, the king turns to the youngest and only living son, whom the mother counsels in their native tongue: "My son, have pity upon me, that bore thee nine months in my womb, and gave thee suck three years, and nourished thee, and brought thee up unto this age. I beseech thee, my son, look upon heaven and earth, and all that is in them: and consider that God made them out of nothing, and mankind also: So thou shalt not fear this tormentor, but being made a worthy partner with thy brethren, receive death, that in that mercy I may receive thee again with thy brethren" (2 Mc 7:27–29).

These passages show that faith in the mercy of God the Creator was not just an intellectual exercise; *believers* held it so strongly that they would give up their lives before denying the laws and the faithfulness of God. Perhaps we could ask whether their faith made sense and whether a family should die for refusing to eat pork. The mother and her sons held true because they believed in a truth beyond them, a truth that lays the very foundations of modern science.

The same conviction was defended in early Christianity. The beginning of the universe cannot be proved by empirical demonstration but by deductive reasoning. It is a rational conclusion outside the bounds of science, with rational consequences to our lives, to hold that there must be a beginning in time. This was a question early Church Fathers addressed, and they addressed it because they had to communicate with other cultures as Christianity spread. The Greeks, like other ancient cultures, saw the circularity in the heavens, in the seasons, and in life as evidence that the cosmos itself was eternally cycling. The observation of cycles led many of them to posit that the cosmos was a living organism or god-being from whom the cosmos emanated eternally. There were disagreements about free will and morality. If the cosmos cycles eternally, then all that happens in a person's lifetime has happened before and will happen again.

In ancient Greece, the idea of an eternally cycling cosmos was called the Great Year. This concept referred to (as expressed in contemporary terms) the period of one complete cycle of the equinoxes around the ecliptic, about 25,800 years. Plato called it the "perfect year" because it marked the length of time it took for the celestial bodies and the stars to return to their original positions.

St. Justin Martyr (ca. AD 100–165) rejected pantheism in his *First Apology*. "Stoics (a school of Greek philosophy) teach that even God Himself shall be resolved into fire, and they say that the world is to be formed anew by this revolution; but we understand that God, the Creator of all things, is superior to the things that are to be changed."[29] In his *Second Apology to the Roman Senate*, he explained that the doctrine of eternal cycles contradicted the concept of morality. "For if they say that human actions come to pass by fate, they will maintain either that God is nothing else than the things which are ever turning, and altering, and dissolving into the same things . . . or that neither vice nor virtue is anything."[30]

Athenagoras (ca. AD 133–190) taught that Christians "distinguished God from matter" and that "matter is one thing and God another, and that they are separated by a wide interval, for the Deity is uncreated and eternal."[31] He also taught that the world was "an instrument in tune, and moving in well-measured time," and that the Deity is the only one who deserved worship because He gave the world "its harmony, and strikes its notes, and sings the accordant strain."[32] Athenagoras noted that failure to realize this distinction led people to inconsistencies about the origin of the world. "Neither, again, is it reasonable that matter should be older than God; for the efficient cause must of necessity exist before the things that are made."[33]

As Christianity spread rapidly throughout the Roman Empire, Christian thought and fundamental characteristics of Greek science began to unite. Clement of Alexandria (died AD 215) taught in Alexandria where the first school of Christian thought emerged, and he also refuted paganism and pantheism. His student was Origen (ca. AD 182–251). Clement and Origen had to both communicate the teaching of the New Covenant to the faithful and to serve as apologists to the pagans. They had to address pagan cosmology.

In his *Exhortation to the Greeks*, Clement taught that idol worship bound the intellect to the blind forces of nature. "Why, in the name of truth, do you show those who have put their trust in you that they are under the dominion of 'flux' and 'motion' and 'fortuitous vortices'? Why, pray, do you infect life with idols, imagining winds, air, fire, earth, stocks, stones, iron, this world itself to be gods?"[34] Clement urged for a more confident attitude toward nature, a view of a world created by a rational Creator. "How great is the power of God! His mere will is creation; for God alone created, since He alone is truly God. By a bare wish His work is done, and the world's existence follows upon a single act of His will. . . . Let none of you worship the sun. Let no one deify the universe; rather let him seek after the creator of the universe."[35]

Origen tried in his *De Principiis* (*On First Principles*) to synthesize Christianity with pagan and Eastern ideas of the cosmos, but he could not see how an eternally cycling cosmos was possible. "So therefore it seems to me impossible for a world to be restored for the second time, with the same order and with the same amount of births, and deaths, and actions . . . "[36] Origen also noticed that such an idea was in conflict with revelation. The events of biblical and salvation history world be repeated over and over again if the world endlessly cycled. He also pointed out that in an eternally cycling cosmos there could be no free will because ultimately everything is predetermined: "For if there is said to be a world similar in all respects (to the present), then it will come to pass that Adam and Eve will do the same things which they did before: there will be a second time the same deluge, and the same Moses will again lead a nation numbering nearly six hundred thousand out of Egypt . . . a state of things which I think cannot be established by any reasoning, if souls are actuated by freedom of will, and maintain either their advance or retrogression according to the power of their will."[37]

Origen, like many of the early Church Fathers, demonstrated the depth of his conviction by martyrdom.[38] The worldview of the Bible and of Christianity was not merely a philosophical outlook; it was a pervasive conviction that was kept pure and protected at any price because the faithful held it *as true*.

If we hold firm to our faith as strongly as the prophets, the biblical authors, the sons and mother in the Second Book of Maccabees, and the Church Fathers did, there is no scientific conclusion in any place or time that could shake our faith. We can "look upon heaven and earth, and all that is in them," not deifying the universe but seeking after the Creator of it, for we know who "balanced the foundations of the earth."

CHAPTER 5

IS THE ATOMIC WORLD THE REAL WORLD?

THE JOURNEY INTO THE ATOM

This ancient appreciation for creation is important in modern times because such a view is foundational to science itself, although it is rarely articulated in scientific circles because the assumption seems obvious. For example, the word "created" appears in the advanced placement level textbook published by Pearson Education (2015 edition). In a discussion about the Big Bang and the nuclear synthesis (formation) of the elements, the book states: "The lightest elements—hydrogen and helium along with very small amounts of lithium and beryllium—were formed as the universe expanded in the moments following the Big Bang. All the heavier elements owe their existence to nuclear reactions that occur in stars. The heavier elements are not all created equally, however."[1] Scientists view the physical realm as a consistently interacting totality, a creation. A scientist must not view the world as a mythological god-being or organism of unpredictable volition but an entity endowed with order and physical laws.

Today we understand much more about all that is in the earth, and we describe it in terms of the atom and its subatomic particles. The atom is the central particle in science, and that is why chemistry is the central science and why I think it is critical to review what we know about the atom in the modern faith-and-science dialogue. Everything around you is made of chemicals—of atoms moving, bonding, and absorbing and releasing energy according to the laws of nature. The home where you live? The desk where you sit? The clothes you wear? The air you breathe? All of it is made of atoms. Your body? It is composed of small, linear, simple, complex, and fleeting organizations of inorganic and organic assemblies made of atoms.

But how small is an atom? A diamond is solid carbon. Carbon has an atomic mass of 12.011 grams per mole. A mole is 6.02×10^{23} particles. One carat is equivalent to 0.20 grams, so we are talking about 1.00×10^{22} atoms of carbon in a one-carat diamond. A quintillion is 10^{18}, so another way to express this figure would be 10,000 quintillion atoms. But that is not really helpful because the human mind cannot easily grasp such a large number without perspective. Think of our journey into minuteness like this: Earth's population is about 7 billion people, so if we could shrink all the people in the world together to replace the atoms of a one-carat diamond, there would be more than 1.4 trillion Earth populations in that diamond.

That is still not very helpful since it is hard to imagine 1.4 trillion groups of 7 billion people, but at least it highlights the fact that we are talking about unimaginably small scales, scales so small that the classical mechanics we intuitively understand from our daily lives no longer apply. It might not seem that anything happening on such small scales is significant, but the atomic realm underlays our macroscopic experience.

We are familiar with the behavior of matter on the macroscopic level. We can see, smell, taste, and touch it, but when we enter the atomic world we are pulled into a strange and unfamiliar landscape. There are protons, which have a +1 charge and a mass of 1.673×10^{-24} grams. The atoms of each element have a unique number of protons, such that the individual elements can be lined up on the periodic table of elements in whole-number succession. Neutrons have no charge but are very, very nearly the mass of a proton. A neutron has a mass of 1.675×10^{-24} grams. Electrons have a −1 charge and are 1/1836th the mass of a proton at 9.109×10^{-28} grams. The protons and neutrons make up the nucleus, and the electrons reside around it in orbitals.

WHAT STUDENTS LEARN ABOUT ATOMS

High-school chemistry students learn about the history of the atom, from the conception of Democritus in ancient Greece to more than 2,000 years later when John Dalton formulated his theory that all elements are composed of tiny indivisible particles that combine in simple, whole-number ratios to form compounds. The search for more fundamental particles continued into the nineteenth and twentieth centuries with the discovery of electrons by J. J. Thomson in 1897, the calculation of the mass and charge of electrons by Robert A. Millikan in 1909, and the discovery of the nucleus and protons by Ernest Rutherford in 1911.

Students are led to Niels Bohr and his planetary atomic model of 1913. Instead of visualizing the atom as a dense, positively charged nucleus with a cloud of electrons moving around it, Bohr proposed that electrons are found only in specific orbits around the nucleus at fixed energy levels. Electrons, the students are taught, can jump from one energy level to another, and a quantum of energy is required for these jumps. Then they learn that the Bohr model of the atom was incomplete.

A high-school textbook might explain that an atom is mostly empty space, and that if the Houston Astrodome, which occupies nine acres, were a 3-D model of the atom, the nucleus would be the size of a marble suspended in mid-air in the very center. But there will hardly be a mention about why the positively charged protons stick together in the nucleus rather than fly apart while the attraction between opposite charges is the reason given for why the electrons orbit the nucleus. There will be no explanation for why more than 99 percent of the atom's mass is in the nucleus, no reason given for why the mass ratio of the electron to the proton is so small, yet the charge is the same magnitude. Those questions generally require higher-level concepts.

High-school students learn how to write electron configurations that dictate the organization of the periodic table, which contains all the elements we know of in the universe, using two rules: the Pauli exclusion principle (no more than two electrons in one atomic orbital) and Hund's rule (electrons occupy orbitals to maximize the number of electrons with the same spin).

While one may need a doctorate in physics to grasp and navigate the equations in quantum mechanics, the results of quantum mechanics are seen on the periodic table. That is how it is ordered. The periodic table is the bridge from the quantum world to human-scale reactions just as the mole is the bridge from invisible to visible amounts of matter. One has but to marvel at the periodic table to know that a wise and intelligent God has "ordered all thing in measure, and number, and weight" (Wis 11:21).

Then high-school students learn about light, the Heisenberg uncertainty principle, electromagnetic radiation, and atomic spectra. They are told that each element has a unique spectroscopic "fingerprint" because each element has a unique number of protons and therefore a unique configuration of electrons to absorb quanta of light, move to higher energy levels, and relax to lower levels while emitting light. They are told that much of the composition of the universe is known through the study of atomic emission spectra from the stars. Thus, before becoming adults, children are exposed to the mysteries of the atomic realm, from the historical models to quantum models and from the elements to the stars.

Students are introduced to the wave-particle duality of electromagnetic radiation (light), which is hard to wrap your head around. When photons that travel in waves are emitted from atoms, there is evidence that they behave both as a wave and a particle. In 1801, the physicist Thomas Young put a card with a single slit and then a card with a double slit in front of a beam of light. He observed an interference pattern on the screen beyond the cards and attributed this to an interference pattern due to wave motion. Over a century later in 1905, Einstein proposed that light also consists of packets of energy called photons. Since the late 1880s, scientists had known that higher energy blue light caused electrons to emit from a metal surface whereas lower energy red light would not. Einstein's photoelectric effect model explained this behavior in terms of photon particles. Photons of blue light have more energy than photons of red light.[2]

The discussion of atomic spectra and wave-particle duality introduces quantum mechanics. What is a quantum? What is quantum mechanics? It seems a lot of people hear the word "quantum" and think of the world of fuzzy probabilities, but the word is derived from classical Latin and actually refers to "something that has quantity."[3] In 1900, Max Plank proposed that atoms release or absorb energy in small, fixed amounts, and he called a single packet a "quantum."

Chemistry textbooks compare this concept to stair steps and inclined planes to show the difference in quantized changes vs. continuous changes in energy.[4] If you move up an inclined plane, your potential energy increases continuously; you could stand anywhere along the slope. If you ascend stairs, your potential energy can only increase in quantized increments because you cannot stand between steps. Quantum theory was based on this idea that matter at the atomic level gains and loses quantized energies.

In 1924, Louis de Broglie postulated that energy could behave as if it were a stream of particles, having a wave-like motion. Then Werner Heisenberg proposed that this dual nature of matter means, in principle, we cannot know the momentum and location of subatomic particles, particularly electrons, simultaneously. This is known as the "uncertainty principle." In 1926, Erwin Schrödinger devised a "wave function" equation that integrates the wave-particle duality to describe the behavior of the electron.

Students are taught that this quantum mechanical model determines the "allowed energies" an electron can have and the probability of finding electrons in various locations around the nucleus. Still today, scientists speak of the *probability* that the electron can be found at a certain location rather than in terms of knowing where the electron is exactly located.[5]

What comes next? In college, science students go on to study the quantum mechanical model in more detail by deriving the equations. They learn *how* Louis de Broglie postulated the wave nature of electrons and demonstrated mathematically that all matter has wave-like properties. They learn that standing waves can be used to describe electron orbitals in Schrödinger's wave function and operator equation.

They learn about Max Planck's constant, Albert Einstein's photon, the mathematics of Heisenberg's uncertainty principle, quantum numbers, electron spin, nuclear charge, and once again the order of the periodic table, but with the deeper insight gained by having worked through mathematical derivations.

To really appreciate the orchestration, you have to hold pencil to paper and step your way through la-la-land systems with their wave functions, eigenvalues, Hamiltonian operators, rigid rotors, and two o'clock in the morning bags of potato chips. Chemistry majors take physical chemistry, a notoriously challenging course, and dive deeper into the equations of quantum chemistry. In chemistry, phenomena at the atomic level—energy levels and properties of atoms and molecules—are understood and calculated with quantum mechanics. In my education, we learned how to calculate electronic orbitals of the hydrogen atom, which contains one proton and one electron, knowing that extending those calculations to atoms with two or more electrons was much more difficult. We learned how the calculus used in quantum mechanics helps us understand ionization potential, electron affinity, atomic size, and again—because it amazes me—the entire periodic table. The order discovered among the elements was so reliable that missing elements on the periodic table were predicted to exist, and then found.

I am reviewing these basics because it seems they are forgotten in the faith-and-science dialogue. There is order and symmetry in the universe, enough to inspire a person to kneel down and weep for joy—and young people learn about it in basic science classes. If we want to inspire young people to love science, we should tell them where all the order came from. Without faith, science class is a rather meaningless exercise.

I remember also being fascinated at the symmetry in molecules and how asymmetry determines whether a molecule has a dipole moment, which is related to the physical reason we can live on Earth. A dipole moment is a separation of charge arising in a molecule because the atoms in the molecule share electrons unequally, kind of like two children playing with a toy. In symmetrical molecules, there is no dipole moment; they are nonpolar. Water is a polar molecule (a dipole as it has two poles) because its structure is bent, giving a slightly negative charge (more electrons) on the oxygen atom and a slightly positive charge (fewer electrons) on the hydrogens. This dipole moment explains why water is the universal solvent; why water can exist as a solid, liquid, or gas in a relatively narrow range of temperatures; and why ice has a lower density than water. All of these properties are critical for life on Earth. Our bodies are mostly water and can dissolve the substances necessary for life. Because ice floats, there is life in the lakes and oceans. So you could say that quantum mechanics reveals to us the higher symmetry of why we can live on Earth.

If we mention the four fundamental forces at work in the universe—the strong force, the weak force, the electromagnetic force, and the gravitational force—we have entered the Standard Model of particle physics. Of course, there is no such dividing line in reality. The switch of disciplines reflects that we have traversed vast amounts of knowledge with the mention of three forces. Interestingly, these forces are better thought of as interactions because they do not exist independently of yet smaller particles.

The strong nuclear force is the force that holds protons and neutrons together in the nucleus. The weak nuclear force is responsible for radioactive decay and also limited in range to subatomic particles. The electromagnetic force is many times stronger than gravity and is a physical interaction between electrically charged particles affecting the processes in chemical reactions. High-school textbooks now include a description of the Standard Model, at least the part about the four forces because the discussion begins to explain why protons do not fly apart in the nucleus and why electrons orbit the nucleus without falling into it.

Known elementary particles are particles in which no further substructure is known; they are grouped as mass particles and force particles. It is instructive to review these briefly, only to provide some appreciation for the details that have emerged in modern science with experiments done in particle accelerators.

To summarize these, I refer to the Halliday, Resnick, and Walker *Fundamentals of Physics* college textbook because I did not learn these names and categories in graduate school back in the 1990s.[6] Today there are several hundred known particles organized into the Standard Model. The particles are classified into three main categories: (1) fermions and bosons, (2) hadrons and leptons, and (3) particles and antiparticles.[7]

Fermions are named after Enrico Fermi who, along with Paul Dirac in the 1920s, described statistical laws that govern identical particles that follow the Pauli exclusion principle. Fermions thus follow this principle; only a single particle can be given a quantum state within the atom. On the contrary, any number of bosons can occupy a quantum state. Bosons are named for Satyendra Nath Bose who, along with Einstein also in the 1920s, discovered statistical laws for these particles. Bosons can compile into a low-energy quantum state to produce a low temperature, very dense condensate (sort of like one big atom) called a Bose-Einstein condensate.[8]

Particles are also classified according to the forces acting on them. Gravity affects all particles, but negligibly for subatomic particles. Electrically charged particles are acted upon by the electromagnetic force that governs chemical reactions at the atomic level. The weak force is involved in nuclear decay. At the subatomic particle level, the strong and weak nuclear forces apply. The strong force binds hadrons (also called nucleons because they are in the nucleus). To further classify, some hadrons are bosons (also called mesons) and some hadrons are fermions (called baryons).[9]

There are eight baryons forming what is termed the "eightfold way" pattern, proposed by Murray Gell-Mann and Yuval Ne'eman in 1961.[10] These particles were classified according to "strangeness," a term that indeed meant that they were strange when first discovered. The term stuck, but it is also considered a quantum number (S) to define +1, -1, and 0 strangeness. When these particles decay, strangeness is conserved; that is, the initial net strangeness must equal the final net strangeness or the decay does not occur. In the eightfold way pattern, the strangeness is plotted against charge quantum numbers along a sloping axis so that a hexagon with two middle particles appears. The same symmetry appears for the nine spin-zero mesons, but there are three middle particles instead of two.

The point here is that these properties and patterns were observed. In fact, vacancies in the patterns guided researchers to find missing particles much like vacancies in the periodic table guided researchers to find missing elements.[11]

The properties of mesons and baryons are explained by an underlying structure called the "quark model," proposed in 1964 by Gell-Mann and George Zweig. On Earth and in astronomical bodies, quarks are found bound in groups of twos or threes for reasons not fully understood.[12] There are six quark particles called the up, down, charm, strange, top, and bottom quarks, and they are thought to be truly elementary particles with no further underlying structure.

Mesons are quark-antiquark pairs. Baryons are combinations of three quarks. It is interesting to note that the masses of baryons do not equal the sum of the quark particles. The mass of a proton, for example, is much more than the sum of its three constituent quarks. Nearly all of the proton's mass is due to the internal energy of quark motion and the fields that bind quarks together. Hence, the mass of macroscopic objects (like your body or your car) is thought to be primarily due to energy.[13]

The particles the strong force does *not* act upon are called leptons. These include the electron and its neutrino that accompanies it in beta decay. The muon and muon neutrino and tau (discovered by Martin Perl in 1975) and tau neutrino are members of this family. As far as is known, leptons have no internal structure either and no measurable dimension. They are considered truly elementary point-like particles, as are the quarks.[14]

Dirac also predicted in the 1920s that electrons should have a positively charged partner. It is now thought that every particle has a counterpart antiparticle, and when the two meet they annihilate each other. They disappear, their energies combine, and they reappear in other forms. For example, when an electron meets a positron (its antiparticle) the energy forms two gamma-ray photons. Assemblies of antiparticles form antimatter, a term which refers to the nature of the particles and not the absence of mass. According to the 2014 physics textbook I am summarizing, future scientists and engineers may build objects of antimatter although nature does not seem to favor this kind of construction since stars and galaxies seem to be made of matter. The authors wonder why the universe was biased toward matter instead of antimatter in the beginning.[15]

The weak force (which, unlike the strong force, acts on all particles) was a theory developed analogous to the electromagnetic force. There are three "messengers" (carriers) of the weak force, the photon and the W and Z particles. In 1979, the Nobel Prize in physics was awarded to Sheldon Glashow, Steven Weinberg, and Abdus Salam for this theory. The strong force theory has also been developed. These messenger particles are called gluons.

The photon and gluon are thought to be massless while the W and Z particles are extremely (by comparison) massive, and this difference was perplexing. In the 1960s, Peter Higgs and, independently, Robert Brout and François Englert proposed a field that permeates all space.[16] This field essentially breaks the symmetry between the four messenger particles in that they would have no mass without it. The quantum of that field is called the Higgs boson.

The further particle physics delves into matter, the more order and symmetry are found. Scientists expect this, and they expect to find unity. While quantum mechanics, which describes the subatomic world, cannot be unified with the general theory of relativity, the mathematical unification of these theories is sought because it is a reasonable goal. The chapter on quarks, leptons, and the Big Bang in the college physics book I consulted for particle physics ends the chapter on quarks, leptons, and the Big Bang by stating that Einstein had a dream of combining the four named forces of nature into one force whose behavior is understood throughout the atomic and the astronomical realm.[17] Grand unification theories (GUTs) try to combine the strong force with the weak force and electromagnetic force. String theory seeks to add gravity to the unification, but it is still in the speculative stage.

That expectation of unification—and all the ways it has been fulfilled and continues to be fulfilled—is marvelous. "And all such things as are hid and not foreseen, I have learned: for wisdom, which is the worker of all things, taught me" (Ws 7: 21).

LAWS AND MODELS

Models are used in science to probe the unknown, and mental pictures fill in the rest of realms we cannot see directly. The models and mental pictures continually need to be updated with the acquisition of new data. Models are scaffolding, like frames that go up before walls, rooms, and décor are built around them, necessary frameworks for gaining new knowledge.

Dr. Denis Edwards at the Australian Catholic University has promoted the work of the late Fr. William R. Stoeger, S.J., who was an astronomer and theologian at the Vatican Observatory Research Group at the Vatican Observatory in Tucson, Arizona. Fr. Stoeger's distinction between "prescriptive" and "descriptive" laws is (to use Edwards's words) "an important legacy for 21-century theology."[18] Consistent with the system of wills approach I explained in chapter 3, he described created nature as "prescriptive." The word "prescribe," means to ordain, to decree, to assign, to lay down the laws. It would be incorrect, even for a nonreligious scientist, to call mathematical descriptions of nature "prescriptive" because that would mean that the scientist lays down the laws. We call the models that scientists derive "descriptive" in that they describe what we can learn about existing order.

The laws of physics are complete, in that God created a fully interacting totality, but we cannot describe all of those laws, and we may never be able to do so. That point is simple, but it is important in the faith-and-science dialogue because it demonstrates why our models, theories, and descriptive laws are not the ultimate explanation of cause.

The atomic world is the real world, but it is invisible, and therefore, our knowledge of it will always remain incomplete. That seems obvious, but it lays the foundation for the next question about free will.

CHAPTER 6

DOES QUANTUM MECHANICS EXPLAIN FREE WILL?

INDETERMINACY AND DETERMINACY

If you engage in the faith-and-science dialogue, you will very likely be asked about the indeterminacy of quantum mechanics. This question is not difficult to navigate if the system of wills is sorted, and you keep the definitions straight.

The deterministic interpretation holds that *all physical events* in the past, present, and future are caused by effects. If every motion of every particle follows laws of nature, then everything happening now is determined by an initial state of matter. If the initial state had been different, there would have been a different reality today. This view concludes that there is no free will, and even if we feel that we have free will, the fact that a finger snaps exactly when it does is actually determined and predestined by physical law.

This view may seem rather extreme, but if a person thinks that all existence is the physical realm, and the physical realm follows laws of physics, then this is the logical end of that reasoning, especially during the time of classical physics before the development of quantum theory. According to the deterministic argument, free will either requires that the past history of the universe be changed as free agents act, or free will causes matter to break the laws of physics. Notice how the materialistic determinism of classical physics and the eternally cycling cosmic treadmill of ancient mythologies are like the ends of a horseshoe. Even though they are opposite extremes, they lead to the same conclusion that there is no free will.

With the new understanding of quantum theory, a philosophically indeterministic view came into popularity, most notably the Copenhagen interpretation linked to the thought of Niels Bohr and Werner Heisenberg originating at Bohr's Institute for Theoretical Physics at the University of Copenhagen around the years 1925 to 1927. This interpretation is harder to define because it was not clearly defined by the people who defended it. The Copenhagen interpretation, loosely, holds that quantum mechanics is not a scaffolding or model, but is the true nature of reality.

Because quantum mechanics is fundamentally a description of the probability of an electron's location, the Copenhagen interpretation has come to be associated with the concept that physical events are probabilistic and not prescribed, and that in turn has led people to conclude that quantum mechanics alleviates the philosophical problem of free will. The argument in a basic form is that quantum mechanics demonstrates that future events are not absolutely determined by causes but governed by probabilities and are therefore subject to chance, randomness, or choice; hence, quantum mechanics has discovered a space for free will.

Although Einstein helped establish quantum physics in its early years, he could not accept that quantum theory allowed uncertainty to reign in the universe.[1] In a September 7, 1944, letter to Max Born, whose statistical interpretation of the wave function was a key component of the Copenhagen interpretation, Einstein wrote, "You believe in the God who plays dice, and I in complete law and order in a world which objectively exists."[2] You may have heard of this line, which Einstein repeated quite a lot.

The question of determinism and indeterminism is also based on the definitions of those words, so I want to clarify the definitions. The word "determine" can mean how a law directs some end or conclusion, and this is the sense of the word in strict physical determinism; the laws of physics determine what happens from beginning to end. The opposite "indeterminism" refers to this form of the verb and thus the idea that a law does not direct behavior so strictly. However, the word "determine" also means, "to ascertain definitely by observation, examination, [and] calculation."[3] If I determine that a flask holds 100 mL, I have used the verb transitively, and this is the definition I use in chemistry or physics. We can determine the location of a stick. We cannot determine the location of an electron. In this sense, saying that indeterminacy provides an explanation for free will (or anything else) is like saying that our inability to know something is an explanation for it. In other words, it is a nonexplanation.

To tie these definitions to the definitions of laws and models given by Fr. William R. Stoeger discussed in the previous chapter, in the sense that the behavior of matter follows *prescriptive* laws of nature, it is (intransitively) deterministic. In the sense that our models are *descriptive* and cannot fully describe all motion of particles, matter is transitively indeterminate and probabilistic. This middle way to interpret quantum mechanics is consistent with the views of two Catholic physicists I have studied, Fr. Stanley L. Jaki and Dr. Peter E. Hodgson. Jaki and Hodgson both rejected strict physical determinism as Catholics, and they rejected the Copenhagen interpretation as physicists.

In his intellectual autobiography, *A Mind's Matter*, Jaki writes of the Copenhagen interpretation of quantum theory that the misstep is a jump from the operational to the ontological, the presumption that "an interaction that cannot be measured exactly, cannot take place exactly."[4] By this he meant (and elaborated on in his books) that theoretical models should be accepted as useful tools but not taken as the full reality. He was very much against extracting philosophical and theological conclusions from incomplete scientific theories. Jaki also taught that a Catholic should be the "most thorough materialist" because "it should be obvious that a personal Creator, "the ground of all existence," can create a "matter which is capable of carrying out every material process."[5]

In his book *Theology and Modern Physics*, Hodgson explains how the wave function describes average properties of an ensemble of systems and that this "leaves open the possibility that in the future there will be a more detailed theory which will enable the quantum paradoxes to be resolved."[6] Hodgson, a particle physicist, was sensitive to the incompleteness of physical theory, as was Jaki, and he made it clear in his writing. Quantum mechanics, he says, is akin to thermodynamics which describes the properties of a gas in terms of pressure and temperature in that even though we express averages of many molecules, we still think the individual molecules follow determined laws.

High-school students learn about the ideal gas equation, for example. This simple equation mathematically relates pressure, volume, temperature, and amount of a gas to each other. (Remember $PV=nRT$?) The relationships are based on assumptions that chemists know are not true of reality. The equation assumes that molecules of gases are hard spheres that take up no space and never lose energy when they collide. In reality, neither assumption is true. But the equation applies over most conditions because the interactions and volumes of the molecules at most conditions of temperature and pressure are negligible, thus justifying the assumptions. Chemists know they cannot determine what individual gas molecules are doing because the models refer to the behavior of an ensemble of molecules. Nonetheless, they also assume that individual particles actually do follow laws of nature.

Or think about rain. If you were to draw a square foot section in your driveway, in theory, equations could describe the trajectory of all raindrops that fall in a given time period. We assume there is ultimately a cause for one raindrop dropping in one place and another in another place. However, we cannot actually account for every location of every drop, nor can anyone predict where the next raindrop will fall. Like particle motion, weather is also deterministic in the sense that it follows prescriptive laws of physics and indeterministic and probabilistic in the sense that descriptive laws cannot determine or predict every motion of every object.[7]

Quantum mechanics is more interesting still. The problem with predicting trajectories of gas molecules or raindrops is not exactly the same problem as predicting the location of electrons. Classical mechanics can determine and predict the position and motion of objects with good certainty, but quantum mechanics cannot. This difference is due to the vastly different size realms. While we cannot measure the exact location and velocity simultaneously of a soccer ball or a boat because motion implies a constantly changing location, we can approximate the instantaneous velocity or location with high accuracy. You do this anytime you glance at your speedometer in your car. But for a moving electron in the atomic realm, the uncertainty in determining the position is ten times greater than the size of the whole atom, and do not forget that the wave-particle duality of particles suggests that they defy our macroscopic understanding of location.[8]

There is another restriction on measuring the motion of particles at the quantum level; the act of measuring changes the behavior of the particle. Our observations rely on light. If a photon of light (a light particle) collides with an electron for the purpose of measuring its location, the photon changes the path of the electron. It is like approaching a billiard table blindfolded and trying to determine the motion of a ball. If you strike the moving ball with an incident ball, or any other object, you change its path.

INTERPRETING QUANTUM MECHANICS

Like Jaki and Hodgson, I do not see how anyone can conclude that matter follows prescriptive laws at all scales, save at the scale we cannot measure. Whatever particle physicists discover, the rest of us should maintain that, wherever they are, particles follow prescribed laws of nature. I held this perspective even before I converted to Catholicism. As a nonreligious scientist, I relied on order and predictability. However, I considered light as a wave to set up the laser equipment, and I considered light a particle when I calculated the quantum yield of experiments. All the while, I knew there must be more to the truth of things beyond what I worked on, and I relied on the use of intellect and free will even though I did not understand what those spiritual powers meant.

In the view of the system of wills described in chapter 3, *physical determinism only applies to the physical realm, while the total reality includes the natural and the supernatural.* Nature follows its prescriptive (designed) physical laws—even if electrons do not actually occupy an exact location in space and time according to those laws and even if they do, but our descriptive models cannot determine the location. *Free agents* (God, angels, humans) are factors that cause matter to move as well, factors that cannot be accounted for fully in physical equations. It is that simple.

The problem in the debates is that people look for an explanation of free will in physics, and they do not consider any reality beyond physics. Catholics are a "both-and" people. We can both hold that God created an ordered universe down to the smallest particle, and we can also hold that He created rational creatures with free will.

As said before, free will or miracles performed by God do not break laws of nature. They are at home in the laws of nature. Our choices are causes, designed to be that way by God. Free will is followed by the laws of physics not produced by them.

Our actions are not interlocked backwards, as the deterministic argument against free will holds, nor does anyone need to posit that our choices were predicted by physical laws from the beginning of time. If we understand that nature is not the whole of reality, then we do not account for our free will within nature. Free will and intellect are spiritual powers. The right way to interlock all events backwards is to place both miracles and human actions within the whole system of reality and follow them all back to their common origin, which is God. To isolate human free will as a physical system is to miss the fuller context.

In the letter published in *Nature* in 1931 (referenced in chapter 4), Fr. Lemaître defended the notion of a beginning in the "present order of Nature."[9] He wrote of quantum theory and how energy of constant total amount is distributed in discrete quanta. If, as it seemed, the number of distinct quanta is ever increasing, then going back over the course of time should lead to fewer and fewer quanta to a single unique quantum in which all the energy of the universe is packed. The highly unstable, "primitive" atom, he proposed, would divide by "super-radioactive" processes into smaller and smaller atoms. Citing the "principle of indeterminacy," he concluded his note poetically: "The whole matter of the world must have been present at the beginning, but the story it has to tell may be written step by step."[10] It is like the rain shower. The water molecules are following laws of nature, but their story unfolds before us—especially if we open an umbrella or splash through a puddle.

HUMANS AND ASSES

The discussion of free will, then, belongs in the realm of the philosophy and theology of the human person, and that is also appropriate before we turn to the biological sciences. Historically, the Latin word *persona*, after the corresponding use of the Hellenistic Greek *prosopon*, meant a mask on a character in a play or a juridical entity.[11] Christian theologians clarified the meaning of "person" dating back to the third-century writings of Tertullian in *Against Praxeas* and the sixth-century writings of Boethius, a Roman philosopher, as referenced and reviewed by St. Thomas Aquinas in the *Summa Theologiæ*.[12]

St. Thomas explains that "person" was defined by Boethius as "an individual substance of a rational nature." The word was used to help understand the Holy Trinity, though it did not fully explain the Holy Trinity because we have no words to fully do so. The Father, the Son, and the Holy Spirit are divine persons in relation who share fully in the divine nature, united as one God.[13] St. Thomas Aquinas explains the order of procession and relations of the three persons of the Trinity. The Son proceeds from the Father as an act of divine intellect, somewhat the way a word is conceived in the mind. From the Father and Son, the Holy Spirit proceeds as an act of divine will.[14]

In Genesis, God said, "Let us make man to our image and likeness" (Gn 1:26). The *Catechism of the Catholic Church* explains, "The divine image is present in every man. It shines forth in the communion of persons, in the likeness of the unity of the divine persons among themselves. . . . By virtue of his soul and his spiritual powers of intellect and will, man is endowed with freedom, an 'outstanding manifestation of the divine image'" (*CCC*, 1702, 1705). The creature is not equal to the Creator, though. Humans may be rational, but we are not omniscient, almighty, or able to create out of nothing.

The spiritual powers of intellect and will instill in us the desires to love and be loved, to know and be known, to learn and make choices, to seek what is good and abhor what is evil. We are created to desire family and community—*many* persons united as *one* entity. The more people freely give, receive, and search for good, the more they are united, the more they learn, the more the human race progresses, and that is why science alone can never provide us all we need to know. Families are the most intimate reflection of the Holy Trinity: two become one and born of their love is a new person. This is the basis of arguments against laws of man that break these divine laws. They are disordered laws that break the unity of people, families, and societies and diminish the freedom and dignity of each person.

We are made to search for God, as every human culture in recorded history has done. We are made to form communities and to seek just laws, as many cultures have done, even though they have all failed to do it perfectly. This also means that we are made to search for what is true and good and to be united with God in heaven.

The term "freethinking" emerged in the eighteenth century among groups that rejected Christianity. The rationalist sect, prominent from the early eighteenth century, typically capitalized the word as a label for themselves. According to the Freedom from Religion Foundation's current definition, a freethinker is "a person who forms opinions about religion on the basis of reason, independently of tradition, authority, or established belief. Freethinkers include atheists, agnostics and rationalists. No one can be a freethinker who demands conformity to a bible, creed, or messiah. To the freethinker, revelation and faith are invalid, and orthodoxy is no guarantee of truth."[15]

The rejection of Christian doctrine has logical implications just as it did in ancient times. Without acknowledging the soul of man created in the image of God, one has no basis for acknowledging the spiritual powers of intellect and free will. Some modern atheists have followed atheism to its logical conclusion and admitted as much. Dr. Sam Harris, author and neuroscientist maintains, "Free will *is* an illusion."[16] Physicist Dr. Victor Stenger wrote, "Since, as far as physics is concerned, we are all just particles, then this would seem to make free will an illusion indeed."[17] Dr. Stephen Hawking, cosmologist and physicist held (with Dr. Leonard Mlodinow), "It is hard to imagine how free will can operate if our behavior is determined by physical law, so it seems that we are no more than biological machines and that free will is just an illusion."[18]

The views of these men are, of course, more elaborate than short quotes, but the denial of free will is fundamentally based on the denial of the existence of God and the soul. If there is no supernatural realm, there is no soul. There is only the physical body. The brain runs its program like a computer obeying the laws of physics, and consciousness is an emergent property of the brain (never mind that the logical end of the materialistic argument that we cannot reason is that we cannot reason that we cannot reason—no end at all). This reasoning reduces the human person to nothing more than a highly developed animal.

So we should compare humans to animals. Animals take in information through their senses, but they cannot analyze it rationally or synthesize data into abstractions and theories. Animals do not do science, have debates, or publish in journals. They have their created natures, but their souls are not created rational as human and angelic souls are. The understanding that the human person is made in the image and likeness of God with a rational soul and the powers of intellect and free will, is a fuller logic.

To put it another way, in his *Summa Contra Gentiles*, St. Thomas Aquinas gave an example of a conditional proposition, a compound proposition where the truth of one clause depends on the truth of the other clause. He compares man to animal. "If man is an ass, he is irrational."[19] His point is that those quadruped beasts of burden are not created with rational souls as are humans. Logically it follows that if man were but an animal, he would by condition also be irrational, as in not a rational being. Let me add to St. Thomas's conditional proposition: if a man denies the soul, he declares himself an irrational ass.

In this chapter, I have juxtapositioned quantum mechanics alongside the spiritual powers of intellect and freedom of will. Quantum mechanics cannot explain free will because the explanation for free will does not belong to physics. Rather than expending intellectual energy to answer the wrong question, maybe more of it could be directed at the consideration of just how much our free choices affect the medium in which we live.

PART III

QUESTIONS IN THE
BIOLOGICAL SCIENCES

CHAPTER 7

DID WE EVOLVE FROM ATOMS?

WE EVOLVED FROM THE BEGINNING

How and when did life begin? Somewhere, somehow inorganic and organic matter crossed a line of complexity and organization and became a living thing capable of reproducing more organisms, controlling chemical reactions with catalysts and inhibitors, and growing and changing over the course of lifetimes. Science is a spectator of life. Science observes, describes, and sorts life's characteristics, once life starts. Science cheers life on, if science is true to itself, for life created science.

An ongoing Gallup poll begun in the early 1980s follows beliefs about human origins.[1] The poll asks people to pick whether they believe that (1) human beings have developed over millions of years from less advanced forms of life, but God guided this process, (2) human beings have developed over millions of years from less advanced forms of life, but God had no part in this process, or (3) God created human beings pretty much in their present form at one time within the last 10,000 years or so. Consistently over the years the most people (40–47 percent) have responded that they believe God created humans in the present form. Fewer people (31–40 percent) believe that humans evolved with guidance from God, and still fewer (9–19 percent) believe that evolution occurred with no guidance from God. The ambiguous phrasing of the questions aside, people seem to have difficulty with the idea that our bodies evolved from less advanced life forms, let alone from inanimate matter or even from atoms.

Every Christian young person will eventually encounter scientific explanations about our origins and destinies that address deep questions about our existence. Fr. Paulinus F. Forsthoefel, S.J., a geneticist and fellow of the American Association for the Advancement of Science, wrote in the introduction of his 1994 book, *Religious Faith Meets Modern Science*, that he often encountered young men and women at Ohio State, the secular university where he made public appearances as a Fellow of the American Association for the Advancement of Science, who could not justify their religious beliefs when challenged by scientific theories.[2] What did they do? Many abandoned their religious practices.

Twenty years later, students heading off to universities may encounter even more difficult challenges. In 2014, Prof. David P. Barash published an opinion column in the *New York Times* titled "God, Darwin and My College Biology Class."[3] He explains in his essay "The Talk" he gives undergraduate students. If the scientific theories were not challenging enough, he goes further and tells students that as evolutionary science has progressed, the "space" for faith has narrowed. He tells them that we are all animals "produced by a totally amoral process, with no indication of a benevolent, controlling creator." He tells them it is not the duty of science to do the mental gymnastics to reconcile faith and science. On the last claim, I agree that difficult questions posed by science to theology should not be settled in a science class, but if students are not prepared to understand science in the light of faith, they will be left in dismal confusion by the rest of Prof. Barash's teaching. It seems obvious that we evolved from atoms if we are made of atoms, but if we leave the question of our existence at materialism's door, we shut out any deeper meaning and purpose.

Let us step through a broader consideration. We see a single evolutionary step every time we see a baby. Biological evolution is the progression of a series of events by which living organisms accumulate changes over successive generations due to genetic inheritance and adaptive variation. Babies are born to parents, generation after generation. Every child is genetically like its parents but also genetically unique as an individual. As such, every child responds to his or her environment in unique ways, however slight the differences may be. Those environments change over time, further affecting genetic expression.

A son may look more like his mom than his dad. He may have inherited dad's allergies but may grow out of them if the family moves to the country. A daughter may have her mom's long legs so she can run fast, but may also have her dad's brown eyes. Because offspring are not genetically identical to parents, and because offspring do not mature in exactly the same environment as parents, evolution occurs. And evolution involves atoms. These are facts. There ought to be nothing remotely troubling to our faith in considering that life emerged from elements and evolved to the present day.

Now take a mental journey further back in time. Evolution occurs generation by generation. Conceptually, if we followed generations back far enough, we might find the most recent common ancestor, defined as an individual who is a genealogical ancestor of all present-day people. Computational models of human genealogy suggest that this ancestor might have lived a few thousand years ago.[4] If we keep traveling back through ancestry, we can arrive at the first human population some 50,000 to 200,000 years (or longer) ago, but no evolutionary model implies a first pair of human individuals.[5] Evolution is understood in terms of populations overlapping and giving rise to new species.

Even if the remains of the first man were found, there would be no way for radiometric dating, genetic dating, or any other analytical system to ascertain that a particular sample came from the first man. This is because dating techniques rely on comparison. When a new specimen is found, it is compared to other samples that have been found and dated. The genetic molecular clock, which uses the rate at which molecular changes accumulate during the evolution of genes or proteins to estimate the timing of evolutionary events, must be calibrated with independent dates from the fossil record.[6] Radiocarbon dating is the most precise method because carbon 14 has the shortest half-life among isotopes used in radiometric dating. Isotopes with longer half-lives can be used to measure longer timescales at the expense of resolution. Even if there were a technique that could resolve down to a single generation, there would be no way to know if the oldest generation found was the oldest generation ever to be found. Speaking of evolution in terms of individuals is like using a bulldozer to pick up the first grain of sand that ever existed on a beach. Not only is it the wrong tool, it is the wrong expectation because we do not think of beaches in terms of first particles of sand.

But neither can genetics rule out a miracle. So if indeed Adam and Eve began to live, literally, as a fully grown man and woman through a miraculous act of God, science can only shrug and keep on digging. If they came to exist some other way, who can ever know? The digging in science is good, though. There is a lot to learn about the history of life, and it is good that scientists explore our physical origins because whatever they discover about our bodily evolution from atoms tells us more about ourselves.

If we imagine a first man existed, even if we stretch the understanding of evolution and assume a first human existed in a population fractions of a second before any other, then we can ask where he came from. He had to be either created miraculously at some point after conception or conceived in a maternal womb. There are no other options. If we said that he dropped from the sky, we would have to call that a miracle. If we said he was born of a nonhuman, we could call that nonhuman a mother. We are left with the conclusion that a first man started out like the rest of us—a highly organized organism made of atoms—and that description applies whether he began as a zygote (a fertilized egg) or an adult lying on the sand. Either way, we can still ask where those atoms came from.

Atoms constitute the matter that makes us up, and every atom in our bodies came from the earth, whose matter seems to have come from supernovas, whose matter probably came from the earliest moments after the Big Bang. As the universe expanded in the fraction of a second after the event, the lightest elements—hydrogen, helium, and some lithium and beryllium—formed. The rest of the elements formed in stars. A star is born when gravitational forces collapse gases and dust into a nebula. At the dense core of the nebula, the high temperatures cause nuclear fusion (the nuclei of atoms fuse) to form helium, also called hydrogen burning.[7] These fusions release energy—lots of it—and this constitutes most of a star's lifetime, including that of our sun. When the hydrogen supply is nearly gone, there is less hydrogen burning, and the star becomes a red giant. The core of the star contracts, and the exterior regions cool so that the star emits red light.

Using helium as its fuel, the star produces beryllium, which either decays or collides with another helium nucleus. If the unstable beryllium and helium collide, they produce carbon. If the carbon reacts with helium, oxygen forms. Hence, there is a curiously high abundance of the elements (hydrogen, carbon, and oxygen) necessary for life on earth. As the stars cool, they become white dwarfs with even denser and hotter cores. This is when fusion processes produce heavier elements until the core is mostly iron. As the core continues to grow in density, the extreme gravitational forces cause the star to collapse, otherwise known as a supernova explosion. The heavier elements form in these dying moments.[8]

It is fun to consider what journey the particles of our bodies have traversed in the last 4.5 billion years on Earth and through the universe in the last 13 billion years. Did you ever wonder how many other bodies all the uncountable particles in your body have occupied? You and I will never know that answer, but nevertheless the particles that make us up have traveled the universe. What supernova have they come from? What cloud did they touch? What rock did they sit in? What river carried them? What other child held them?

The point of this exercise is to show that a Catholic can both explore what evolutionary science has to reveal and, simultaneously, believe in the existence of Adam and Eve. What a Catholic, or anyone else, cannot do is expect evolutionary science to find them. Catholics should not be grimacing when people say humans evolved from atoms. They should be holding up a finger and adding, "We evolved from the beginning."

THE CHEMICAL ORIGIN OF LIFE

On Ash Wednesday, the minister marks the cross on our foreheads with ashes and says, "Remember, you are dust and to dust you will return." It is a reminder that we are human, that in death our bodies will remain on earth and decay while the souls of the just will go to meet God and wait to be reunited with their glorified bodies through the power of Jesus' Resurrection. We believe this spiritual truth in faith. And we know scientifically that the body decays. We can see it happen, a chemical process by which the complexly structured living body decomposes back to simpler molecules.

The chemical *origin* of life is harder for us to understand. Genesis says, "And the Lord God formed man of the slime of the earth: and breathed into his face the breath of life, and man became a living soul" (Gn 2:7). The biblical statement that "God formed man of the slime of the earth" is consistent with the idea that we were formed from nonliving material. Scientists have studied this process of "chemical evolution," and they consider the origin of life a hypothesis subject to experimental verification since those ideas can be tested in laboratories.

It is funny to recall that there was a time when people did not know how organisms were generated. At one time, natural scientists thought life spontaneously sprang from nonliving material because they saw decayed meat produce maggots, mud produce fish, and grain produce mice. Spontaneous generation was a reasonable explanation for what people observed.[9]

In 1668, an Italian physician named Francesco Redi thought to disprove spontaneous generation by putting decaying meat in both covered and open jars.[10] What happened? The maggots did not appear, of course, in the covered jars, but they did appear in the open jars. So people changed their conclusions to suppose that spontaneous generation might occur from a "vital force" in the air.

In the mid-1800s, Louis Pasteur disproved the spontaneous generation of microorganisms from air. In his experiments, he boiled a nutrient-rich broth to kill all microorganisms.[11] When he exposed the broth to air, nothing happened. No microorganisms were produced. When he added microorganisms into the boiled broth, more microorganisms soon grew. The conclusion, as we well know today, is that living organisms come from other living organisms (not air). This observed law is called biogenesis. Living organisms do not spontaneously appear from nonliving material, and that knowledge has become the cornerstone of biology. It is also the reason why the theory of evolution is foundational to all biological sciences: evolution depends on biogenesis.

Although biologists have accepted the concept of biogenesis for well over 150 years, the experiments above shed no light on how life arose in the first place. There have been other experiments to explore the question of "abiogenesis," the chemical evolution of life from non-living material.[12]

In 1871, Charles Darwin was one of the first scientists to advance a hypothesis about abiogenesis. Darwin is also known as the originator of the theory of evolution. In a letter to a colleague he wrote: "It is often said that all the conditions for the first production of a living organism are now present, which could ever have been present. But if (and oh what a big if) we could conceive in some warm little pond, with all sorts of ammonia and phosphoric salts, light, heat, electricity, etc., present, that a protein compound was chemically formed ready to undergo still more complex changes, at the present day such matter would be instantly devoured, or absorbed, which would not have been the case before living creatures were formed."[13]

Since Darwin's time, radioactive dating studies have indicated that Earth is about 4.54 billion years old. The fossil record indicates that the earliest evidence of life, organisms resembling modern-day bacteria, originated about 3.5 billion years ago. Thus, data indicate there was a period of about a billion years when no life existed on Earth, a "prebiotic" era in scientific terms.[14]

There have been many experiments to probe the steps of this primal abiogenesis, and the studies are ongoing. High-school and college biology textbooks preface discussion of the history of research into the question of primal abiogenesis—the chemical evolution of life from nonliving material—by acknowledging that scientists know it is impossible to determine exactly how life arose on Earth. As a

Glencoe/McGraw-Hill textbook states at the beginning of a discussion on the origin of life, "No one will ever know for certain how life began on Earth."[15] A college biochemistry textbook published by John Wiley and Sons goes into great detail about possible theories, but similarly states in the first chapter on the origin of life that it is "impossible to describe exactly how life first arose."[16]

Scientists form theories about how a living cell *might have arisen* through a series of steps, with each step having some probability of occurring. Simple carbon-containing molecules must have formed. Then those molecules must have organized into complex polymers and then into the three-dimensional proteins, carbohydrates, and nucleic acids essential for life.

Scientists hypothesize that there must have been little or no free oxygen in the atmosphere, because free oxygen could not have been there before the existence of photosynthesizing cells and because an organic compound spontaneously synthesized in the presence of free oxygen would have degraded instantly. The primitive atmosphere might have had water vapor, carbon dioxide, nitrogen, methane, and ammonia.

In the 1930s, a Russian biochemist, Alexander Oparin, hypothesized that life began in the oceans after the sun, lightning, and heat triggered chemical reactions to produce small organic molecules from substances in the air.[17] Then rain, he suggested, might have washed the molecules into the oceans to form the "primordial soup."

In 1949, British molecular biologist John Desmond Bernal hypothesized that life arose in roughly three stages: (1) a chemical evolution from simple molecules found in rocks, water, and air to organic monomers, (2) the organization of these monomers into biological polymers, and (3) the organization of these polymers into structures such as proteins and cells.[18] He thought there might have been first a "chemical evolution" to the first living cell and then a "biological evolution" from that first cell to the biodiversity we find today, also known as the "web of life."

In 1953, two American scientists, Stanley Miller and Harold Urey, simulated Oparin's hypothesis in the laboratory.[19] They mixed water vapor with ammonia, methane, and hydrogen gases and sent an electric current through the mixture (lightning). Then they cooled the mixture (rain) and collected it in a flask. After a week, they found several kinds of amino acids, sugars, and other small organic molecules such as those found in living things. In the 1950s, more experiments were done to show that if amino acids are heated in the absence of oxygen, they can form proteins.

In 1965, another American biochemist, Sidney Fox, showed that heating solutions of amino acids produces short chains of amino acids, which then organize into large, ordered structures with a membrane that can carry out some activities necessary for life, such as growth and division. He called this structure a "protocell."[20]

Even after all this time and with all of these experiments, there is still no "standard model" of the origin of life. No one has actually synthesized a "protocell" from the bottom up. Some researchers, such as Steen Rasmussen, a Danish physicist, and Jack Szostak, a Canadian-American geneticist, are exploring whether a top-down approach might be more useful.[21] They study existing organisms to discern what the minimal requirements are for life. Their research, therefore, involves the study of the production of "artificial life." Still others, such as Romanian-American ecologist John Priscu, study whether life originated in a hot or a cold environment or independently in both.[22]

These theories propose a gradual evolution of life based on the chemical properties of matter favored by (naturally selected by) the primitive Earth's environment. Fundamental to all these scientific studies is the assumption that living things differ from nonliving things primarily in their degree of organization. However, the question of whether all the properties of biological life can be explained by complex organization still remains to be answered.

One might wonder whether these scientific speculations through history are in conflict with Christian beliefs. No, they are not. Scripture says that God created *all things*, living and nonliving, spiritual and material. If living organisms arose from nonliving material because their organization reached a certain necessary complexity for the vital activities of growth and reproduction, this transition can be regarded

as a result of the potentialities with which the Creator endowed creation. If the very first emergence and consequent spread of life was a
series of miracle after miracle outside the order of nature, then science
cannot study those events and turn the knowledge into a scientific
theory. Science is a good way to find what answers we can find, and
scientists, in general, do not spend their hours conjuring up ideas to
dismiss God. The statement "You are dust and to dust you will return"
has a scientific meaning, but one understood properly only in the light
of faith.

CHAPTER 8

ARE CREATIONISM AND INTELLIGENT DESIGN CORRECT?

CREATIONISM

Upon converting and then going public as a Catholic, I quickly encountered two groups of people who confused me: young-Earth creationists and intelligent design theorists. When I did not quickly agree with creationists on some rather fundamental points about the age of the Earth and the evolution of living things after studying the writings of popes and theologians, I was directed to lots of reading material written by creationists to educate myself.

I had great difficulty getting past the opening statements in some of their literature. Let me back up. When I accepted the gift of faith, it was like someone turned the lights on—I could see and understand a fuller reality. I could see science in its greater context of metaphysical, philosophical, and theological truths. As I said before, accepting that God the Father Almighty created heaven and the earth was the most satisfying intellectual assent I have ever made, not a God hypothesis but an understanding that the Symphony Writer and Molecular Designer is Someone real. Though not as a child, I returned to the childlike belief that God made everything.

I understand now why scientists grapple. It is because they are human and must take in observations and data so they can process new information into abstract hypotheses, theories, and laws. Scientists grapple because the scientific method is the only way they can gain knowledge about the physical world. I understand why doing science without acknowledging God felt like turning my back to a chasm. In the light of faith, I can look into the chasm and not fear it. I can see that it is too vast for me or any other human to ever discover all its mysteries, but I can appreciate that discovering a little more truth is better than not even trying. I can be excited about small advances in knowledge without feeling anxious to have all of the answers. I can enjoy a symphony because I can let go of the expectation that I need to know all the details to take in the music. The details are there to be studied, but the beauty is in the music. I had it backwards. On encountering creationists, I could not figure out how they approached either faith or science.

Some of them told me, not in as few words, that unless I accepted their scientific conclusions about cosmology, evolutionary theory, geology, radiocarbon dating, and the Big Bang, I lacked faith. They told me that if I did not read Genesis literally (according to their definition of "literally") my faith was restrained by atheism. Without going into detail, I will just say that to accept their conclusions, a person needs to disregard the scientific community and adhere to their teaching.

It seems people have one of three reactions to creationists. There are those who join creationists's ranks, cite their material, defend their claims, and are certain that anyone who is not a creationist has been led astray by the pervasive atheism of our day. Second, there are those who argue with creationists, refute their scientific points, and engage in drawn-out debates. In the end, the debates (apparently entertaining to some) seem a large waste of time. Third, there are those who hear them out, decide they are incorrect, tolerate their criticism, and mostly remain silent because they are too busy to address the myriad of details. Normally, I sit in the last group, but there is something, I think, that needs to be said, and I am saying it for the sake of anyone else who has been hesitant to speak up about the behavior of creationists.

When I tried to engage creationists with an open mind, in case I was missing something, the ones I directly interacted with were aggressive. If I did not reject evolution, I was labeled an evolutionist. They called me gullible for accepting evolution. I am aware that evolution does not have all of the answers. Any evolutionary biologist will tell you that there is much more to discover. There are creative scientists working on all kinds of ways to expand the theory computationally and physically. Because I accept evolution and am interested in new developments, I was labelled a modernist and a liberal.

The criticism that I lacked real faith was actually painful, and I choose to address this aspect of young-Earth creationism rather than the science because the moral debate is where the greatest harm is done. Accusing people of lacking faith for rejecting any scientific conclusion is a form of violence to the soul. I changed my whole life to become Catholic. Faith is the center of my life, and I order everything in my life around it. My love for Christ and his Church, for our Blessed Mother, for the saints and doctors, for the other Catholics living in our time—all of it—was and still is my center. I do not say this because I am a convert. Christians in communion feel this way all over the world. I have many friends, mentors, and loved ones who take their faith just as seriously as I do.

It was confusing to be accused of having a false faith and to be labeled a danger to the Church because I did not agree with creationists' scientific conclusions. In trying to follow the Church, I read authentic magisterial Church documents, yet I was told that I was not following the "real" Church because I would not throw out my science textbooks, the writings of St. John Paul II and Pope Benedict XVI, and the work of the Pontifical Academy of Sciences to instead uphold creationists as the only true and legitimate authority. When they accused me of dishonestly trying to lead people astray because I still would not bend to their dictates, I decided that was enough.

While I cannot recount every conversation I had, I can cite an example in a book. The 2007 book by Rev. Victor P. Warkulwiz titled *The Doctrines of Genesis 1–11: A Compendium and Defense of Traditional Catholic Theology on Origins* carries the reading line "Everything a Catholic Needs to Know to Uphold the Literal Truth of Genesis 1–11."[1] The author is a priest and holds a doctorate in physics from Temple University, a master of divinity from Mount St. Mary's Seminary, and a master's degree in theology from Holy Apostles College and Seminary. He is a theological reviewer for the Kolbe Center for the Study of

Creation, a young-Earth creationists' group that sponsored his afore-mentioned work. He rejects the theory of evolution because, according to him, it cannot be accommodated by genuine Catholic theology. Yet, he notes, many Catholic scientists and intellectuals have "succumbed to scientism, putting more faith in the reigning paradigms of science than in the words of Sacred Scripture."[2]

He goes on in his book to say that evolution leads people away from the faith because it is atheistic in spirit and meant to be an attack on divine revelation and the existence of God. He cites Pope Leo XIII's 1893 encyclical, *Providentissimus Deus*, to warn that modern science sows confusion in the minds of young people who are not "sophisti-cated" enough to rationalize their way through it: "[F]or the young, if they lose their reverence for the Holy Scripture on one or more points, are easily led to give up believing in it altogether" (*Providentissimus Deus*, 18). He writes that the notion of an earth that is billions of years old has a numbing effect on youth, causing them to push God into the background until he is not relevant in their lives.[3]

I have seen firsthand that this is not true for young people. If you teach them how to responsibly appreciate science in the light of faith, and you teach them about the profound order throughout the uni-verse, they are excited and inspired, and they are equipped to navigate challenges. Likewise, Pope Leo XIII did not seem to be referring to anyone who accepted evolution. He specifically addressed those who make "evil use of physical science" and scrutinize Genesis with the intent of vilifying its contents.[4] The Catholics who accept evolution as a scientific theory are not making "evil use of science" or vilify-ing the contents of Genesis. These are not the people Pope Leo XIII referred to. The Catholics who explore evolutionary science are asking and seeking answers to legitimate questions, often precisely because they want to be able to guide young people. In the same section of the encyclical, Pope Leo XIII reminded the faithful that the sacred writers of Genesis "did not seek to penetrate the secrets of nature, but rather described and dealt with things in more or less figurative language, or in terms which were commonly used at the time" (*Providentissimus Deus*, 18).

Warkulwiz continues that all evidence contrary to evolution is "ignored, shouted down, or dismissed with flimsy arguments" or is flat out suppressed in the same way the truth about abortion is suppressed. He accuses the "evolutionists" of waging a propaganda campaign to silence opposition. He charges Catholic who accepts evolutionary theory of being "too eager to jump on the evolution bandwagon" because they think that by "injecting God into the theory they can free it from its atheistic roots" (theistic evolution). Some Catholics, he says, have become "smitten by a fatal attraction to the theory, as if the idea of God using blind physical forces to bring about the universe and life over eons of time is somehow more awesome and beautiful than God creating at once in a magnificent act of love." Others—he continues the litany of charges against Catholics who accept evolution—are afraid they will appear to be behind the times and opposed to science. Then he writes that all of this has led Catholics to fail at evangelizing because we play the secularist game according to their rules rather than uphold the Catholic theology of origins.[5]

I tried for years to give creationists the benefit of the doubt in charity, and I still think we should treat them with kindness, but if I could put the young-Earth biblical literalists all into a room together and be given a moment to make a plea, I would ask them one question: *Do you care about the harm you do to fellow Catholics and Christians when you wage these accusations?*

Accusing someone of lacking faith for not rejecting evolution is coercive. Accusing people of suppressing truth the same way people suppress the "truth about abortion" is damaging to the reputations of good people. Accusing scientists of waging campaigns to silence the faithful is unwarranted. Accusing Catholics who accept evolution of being gullible, blind followers of atheism is condescending. Telling Catholics who accept evolution that we are responsible for failed evangelization seems like blame shifting. Creationists say they are certain of their position, but their accusations belie their confidence.

The Catholic Church has not advanced any theory of evolution as dogmatic. The recent popes, along with the Pontifical Academy of

Sciences and the vast majority of Catholic scholars, have explored the open question in need of further scholarship.

INTELLIGENT DESIGN

And then I discovered the intelligent design movement. My first thought on hearing that name was that it sounds more like a religious claim than a scientific one. When confronted with that thought in public, intelligent design advocate Dr. Stephen C. Meyer replied, "Contrary to media reports, [intelligent design] is not a religious-based idea, but an evidence-based scientific theory about life's origins."[6] *But what,* I wondered, *is the scientific evidence?* According to intelligent design theorists, certain features of the universe and of living things are best explained by an intelligent cause, not an undirected process such as natural selection acting on random variations; and they claim that they can empirically detect the difference.

Intelligent design theory claims that "there are natural systems that cannot be adequately explained in terms of undirected natural forces and that exhibit features which in any other circumstance we would attribute to intelligence."[7] They make a distinction between nature and design, as if nature were not designed. What is concerning about that claim is that intelligence is defined by the ones who claim they find intelligence. For example, Dr. Stephen Meyer wrote in a 2006 article in the *Daily Telegraph* (UK) that biologists have discovered an "exquisite world of nanotechnology within living cells," something I know well to be true, and they point to those marvels as proof of intelligent design.[8] He also wrote that Dr. Michael Behe points to the flagellar motor and its coordinated function of thirty protein parts (if one of those proteins is missing, the motor does not work) as an example of something that is "irreducibly complex."[9] I agree with such statements as an expression of awe and wonder, but as I explained in chapter 4, design is an all-or-none proposition.

What about the atom? Is not the very foundation of matter irreducibly complex and therefore intelligently designed too, by their definitions anyway? And that is even more confusing. It is as though they roll up their sleeves, stand before God, and tell him whether he did a good job or not. The rock and the rotting wood? "No, not so intelligently designed, God." The gene and the bacterium's flagellar motor? "Why yes, now that is some intelligent work!" I do not know how anyone can escape the conclusion that atoms themselves are designed, not just single atoms but their formation, their subatomic structure, their relation to each other, their rules for bonding.

Intelligent design theorists demonstrate what happens when the system of wills is not kept sorted out, when it is not primarily understood that nature is part of creation and that creation includes more than nature. For example, Dr. William Dembski defends the idea that intelligent design is a valid scientific hypothesis in his 2004 book, *The Design Revolution: Answering the Toughest Questions about Intelligent Design*.[10] He offers an explanation in the middle of the book about how an "unembodied designer" might interact with matter at the subatomic level.[11] That explanation is needed in order for intelligent design to be credible as a scientific theory because there has to be some explanation for the designer to act in the material realm. I realize Dembski's book was written more than ten years ago at the time of my writing this book, but the arguments for intelligent design, in my opinion, hinge on this question just as Descartes's mind and body duality hinged on the pineal gland.

Dembski first posits that an unembodied designer who moves particles is not a logically incoherent claim for physical science. Although physical mechanisms are a sufficient explanation for the motion of particles, he says, an unembodied designer could also intervene to move particles. So far, this point is consistent with a belief in a Creator who both holds everything in existence and intervenes to work miracles (the system of wills). However, Dembski notes, an unembodied designer inserted into the *scientific* explanation is an arbitrary intrusion. I agree. We do not need to add God into science to prove design.

Instead of leaving the argument there and noting that such predictions are beyond the capabilities of physical science—which I suppose would undermine the basis of intelligent design *as a physical science*—he goes further. Dembski claims that the designer might be in the business not of moving particles but of "imparting information."[12]

Similar to the way some theorists invoke quantum mechanics as an explanation for free will in that they try to explain how our minds can interact with our bodies, Demski relies on the quantum as an explanation for imparting design. "It is here," he says, "that an indeterministic universe comes to the rescue."[13]

According to Dembski, "nature moves its own particles," but the designer imparts information at the quantum level (as if the designer of nature had no hand in nature moving its own particle).[14] Dembski speculates that perhaps "zero-energy" events could be the conduit for intelligent design in our "indeterministic" universe.[15] What does he mean by "zero-energy"? He explains that since there is no upper limit to the wavelength of electromagnetic radiation, there is consequently no lower limit to the frequency and thus no lower limit to the energy required to supposedly "impart information."[16]

This needs explaining. If you draw a transverse wave, it is easy enough to see that if you stretch out the wave (wavelength increases) the number of waves per second (frequency) will decrease. This is an inversely proportional relationship, just like with making lemonade. Assuming you use one cup of sugar and one cup of lemon juice in a half-gallon of water, if you add another gallon of water, the concentration is diluted. As volume increases, concentration decreases. Saying there is a theoretical zero-energy at the theoretical upper limit of radiation wavelength is like saying that if you diluted the lemonade infinitely with water, you could find a point where the lemon and sugar disappear. Such theoretical limits shed no understanding on physical reality in a question about an intelligent designer.

Nevertheless, in this upper limit wavelength, zero-energy ideal, Demski says the unembodied designer could tell matter what to do without imparting energy. This reasoning is highly speculative and completely untestable.

Furthermore, we need to start the reasoning before we get to science. To "create" means to bring into being, to cause to exist.[17] To be created means to be related to God through ontological dependence. Anything created points inherently to the Creator. There can be no absolute chance or randomness in a cosmos divinely governed by order down to the tiniest particle. We do not need to search for some physical mechanism by which God tells matter what to do.

There is a story that a little old lady once told a cosmologist that the universe was standing on the back of a turtle. When he asked her what the turtle was standing on, she said, "Another turtle." He kept asking, and she kept answering, "Turtles all the way down." What we should be saying is this: the universe is thoroughly designed—all the way, in all dimensions, consistent with St. Thomas Aquinas's fifth way. "Therefore some intelligent being exists by whom all natural things are directed to their end; and this being we call God."[18]

I am concerned that teaching people, especially children, that they can distinguish between guided and unguided processes and designed and undesigned objects teaches them that God did not create "all things," or that he created some things unintelligently, or that we are the judges of God's intelligence. One ought to shudder at such thoughts. It is enough to say that God Almighty created everything, and science is the study of his handiwork, with the strong admonishment that understanding some science does not make one omniscient. Like I said, design is an all-or-none proposition. If you are going to proclaim an intelligently designed universe, you have to start there in faith, lest your proclamations be limited to your own intelligence.

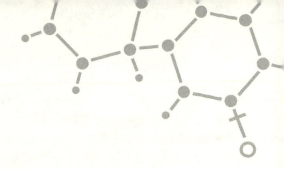

CHAPTER 9

CAN A CHRISTIAN ACCEPT THE THEORY OF EVOLUTION?

A DINNER PARTY CONVERSATION

A man is invited to dinner with friends of his wife's. He knows the host, of course, and a few other guests, but he does not know everyone. He strikes up a conversation with another gentleman after they share a knowing chuckle at their obsession with their mobile phones. Both are checking for messages from the babysitter and quickly checking the game scores for the Monday night football game they could be watching. Their wives are with the other ladies, chatting in the living room. They make small talk about the difficulties of getting out on a Monday night and about how the blue cheese–stuffed colossal green olives served for appetizers go well with the unoaked Chardonnay. They are not really interested in the olives or the dinner party. With nothing else to talk about, one man decides to ask the other about his work.

"Well, I am an evolutionary biologist. I specialize currently in genomic studies of Neanderthal ancestry in humans."

The first man is somewhat taken aback. "Oh, how interesting. Say that again—you study genes of what?"

"Neanderthal ancestry. Yes, that usually gets a brow raised."

"In humans?"

"In humans. Our genetics suggest that modern man and *Homo neanderthalensis* bred once upon a time. *Homo sapiens* and Neanderthals, we believe, share a common ancestor from Africa more than 500,000 years ago. The Neanderthal ancestors migrated to Europe and Asia. The modern human ancestors stayed in Africa until about 100,000 years ago and then migrated. So for a time both species coexisted in Eurasia. Scientists have now sequenced the Neanderthal genome in DNA taken from fossils. The genetic material suggests that our ancestors interbred some, but not a lot, with Neanderthals before Neanderthals went extinct about 30,000 years ago.[1] They bred about 37,000 to 86,000 years ago.[2] Eurasian genomes today are 1 to 4 percent Neanderthal DNA. I'm interested in how this bit of DNA that stayed with us down through time has affected the current human population. Sorry, I tend to go on and on when asked about work. Clearly, I don't get out enough." He winds himself down with a self-effacing grimace.

The other man stares at his new acquaintance, having a conversation with himself in his head instead of speaking. Well, how do you like that? Here's a guy standing right in front of me, a dad, a football fan, a scientist, a professional, an expert, and he's saying this in all seriousness. Humans and Neanderthals had sex and made babies! And what am I? Descended from apes? The staring man stares at his wine glass, kind of embarrassed because he does not know what to say; then he stares at the scientist's glass and wonders if maybe he is drunk; then he stares at the ugly colossal olive with the lump of cheese goop in it. Then he checks his phone again, but suddenly remembers it is his turn to talk. He decides he may as well state the obvious.

"Well, that's remarkable."

The scientist takes this response as a cue to continue. "Yes, quite! Researchers found Neanderthal ancestry at specific loci in the genomes of people living today. I am interested in what benefits those loci give to modern humans. Mating with Neanderthals was probably both helpful and harmful. The hybrid babies were probably too infertile to maintain a lineage, but some of the genes stayed with some of us, maybe the genes that allowed humans to live in climates colder than in Africa. Neanderthals were quite robust and well adapted to cold climates. Researchers have identified a set of genes that affect the keratinocytes in modern human skin and hair cells. There's potentially a medical benefit to understanding our ancestral genetics better."[3]

Knowing it would be rude to keep repeating that Neanderthal-human sex is remarkable, the staring man decides to weigh in with veracity. "I'll be honest, man, I've never heard of anything like that. It's shocking to think humans and Neanderthals mated. It's even shocking, to me, just to imagine Neanderthals existed at all. I don't really have a problem accepting evolution, I guess, but to meet someone who speaks about nonhuman prehumans, or whatever they are called, so matter-of-factly is just rattling."

"I get that a lot when I am outside my circle of colleagues. I guess I forget not everyone is used to thinking about our ancestry this way. Can I ask you something?"

"Shoot."

"Are you religious?"

"Yes, I am. That's why what you're talking about sounds so otherworldly to me. I was just teaching my son about Adam and Eve yesterday after church. One man and one woman from whom we are all descended, and all that. What you're saying is so different, it's like we live in two different realities."

"Does it bother you that people like me talk about humans evolving from primates?"

"It does. I don't know what to do with that information . . . but I don't doubt that you are serious and intelligent."

"Thanks for saying that. I am not religious. No reason really. I was raised in a home that wasn't religious. We weren't antireligious, but it just wasn't a thing. For me, hearing about Adam and Eve and the Do-Not-Touch tree sounds otherworldly. I wouldn't even know where to begin to try to verify such a story."

"Touché, dude. Hey, looks like dinner's about to begin. Let's eat and hope to catch the end of the game."

The two men go back to their wives and share an enjoyable evening together, football notwithstanding. Both have much to think about, but there is probably less for the nonreligious scientist. The biologist does not have much use for thinking about Genesis. He does not need to think about Genesis for his work—so he assumes—nor does he need to think about it for his life as a husband and father. He does not think

Adam and Eve ever really existed, so he has little reason to worry about explaining their story with the story line of his work. Nonetheless, he admits to himself every once in a while, when he allows himself to go there, that the stories of human origins he tells his son at bedtime are ultimately flat: "Son, you and I are offspring of offspring, points on a network of evolution leaving behind offspring who are points on the network of evolution." His science has no accounting for meaning and purpose, and nothing makes that void as troublesome as being a parent, but perhaps his encounter with the other father has planted a seed.

The believer has much more to think about in the moment. Truly, he has the sense that it would have been better never to have known about Neanderthals at all. Period. Nada. Zilch. They totally mess up the vision he has in his mind, and they mess up what he thought he accepted about evolution. The Church does not teach a literal, six-day-creation interpretation of Genesis. The thing is, he had not really thought evolution posed any difficulty for his faith, until suddenly he found himself unsure how to connect this rather shocking information about Neanderthals with what he teaches his son. If there were Neanderthals, there were others, but what others? He decides to look it up and learn more about it in the coming weeks and months. His son will surely ask him about evolution someday, and the father wants to be ready with answers.

What is a person of faith supposed to do with the very legitimate-sounding information that Neanderthals and humans bred? One reaction is to reject all of it and refuse to think about it. Many people do that. They guffaw at the notion that humans evolved from apes (more accurately, apelike creatures), they call it nonsense, and they decide they are done with the topic. I strongly warn against this attitude, especially if other people look to you for guidance. You will stifle curiosity about a legitimate subject of discourse and set those other people up for overwhelming confusion if they ever actually sit down and learn the least bit about evolutionary science.

Another reaction would be to remain open to the scientific conclusions, even if you are not sure what to make of them. The science of evolution is not simple. It is an entire field of study, with methods, terminology, and established theories. New papers about new discoveries and ideas regarding the history and future of life are constantly being published. Devotion to science can, of course, go to extremes if people think they know more than they know or take current scientific consensus as hard truth that cannot be questioned. We know this happens. It has been labeled scientism (see chapter 2). Such a heavy dependency on science is foolish because it demands more of science than science can give. But remaining open to the ongoing discoveries of science is prudent.

The best reaction is to remain curious about science, but also to maintain some objectivity where truth is certain. Let us unpack it.

REAL AND LITERAL

As Catholics, we hold divinely revealed truths as certain dogma, certain in the sense of deserving total assent in faith to what God has revealed for the sake of our salvation. Since the topic of evolution is so controversial, probably the most controversial faith-and-science topic of our times, it is critical for us to have a solid grasp of the dogmas that cannot be negotiated or denied. It is also critical that we know how to distinguish between dogma and opinion. The Church carefully articulates every expression of dogmatic truth. These are truths that science can never deny, although science may help us understand what they mean. Remembering the axiom "truth cannot contradict truth" (*Providentissimus Deus*, 23), read the decisions of the Pontifical Biblical Commission in 1909:

> a) The first three chapters of Genesis contain narratives of real events . . . , no myths, no mere allegories or symbols of religious truths, no legends.
> b) In regard to those facts, which touch the foundations of the Christian religion . . . , the literal historical sense is to be adhered to. Such facts are, *inter alia*, the creation of all things by God in the beginning of time and the special creation of humanity.

c) It is not necessary to understand all individual
words and sentences in the literal sense. . . . Passages
which are variously interpreted by the fathers and by
theologians may be interpreted according to one's
own judgment with the reservation, however, that one
submits one's judgment to the decision of the Church,
and to the dictates of the Faith.

d) As the Sacred Writer had not the intention of rep-
resenting with scientific accuracy the intrinsic constitution of things and the sequence of the works of
creation but of communicating knowledge in a popular way suitable to the idiom and to the pre-scien-
tific development of his time, the account is not to
be regarded or measured as if it were couched in language which is strictly scientific. . . .

e) The word "day" need not be taken in the literal
sense of a natural day of twenty-four hours but can
also be understood in the improper sense of a longer
space of time.[4]

Notice the statement that Genesis contains narratives of real
events and the statement that it is not necessary to understand all sentences in the literal sense. A narrative is an account of events, but there
is room for further development and interpretation. The guidance is
clear that the creation of all things by God in the beginning of time
and the special creation of humanity must be taken literally. The Biblical Commission also states that the sacred writer was not writing
scientifically to give a fact-by-fact sequential account of the "intrinsic
constitution of things," but was writing in a "popular way" to communicate knowledge. This statement suggests that Genesis 1–3 is a real
story that is not intended to be understood literally.

It is helpful to distinguish between "real" and "literal." The word
"real" means to actually exist. Stemming from the postclassical Latin
realis, the word simply means "actual."[5] The word "literal" comes from
postclassical Latin *litteralis* (also *literalis*), but it relates to letters, books,

or literature.[6] Theologically, it is defined as "of or relating to the 'letter' of a text, obtained by taking words and passages in their primary or usual meaning, without regard to any underlying significance, or allegory." "Literal" can also mean "actual," but in the concrete sense as opposed to any figurative or metaphorical sense. The "letter" in the definition means the precise words, terms, or strict verbal interpretation of a statement.

Even creationists do not take every phrase in Genesis literally because the literal interpretation is not as full as the real interpretation. For example, in the third chapter, Eve sees that the tree is good to eat, fair to the eyes, and delightful to behold; she takes the fruit and eats it. Then she gives it to her husband, and Adam eats it. In verse 7, the text says, "And the eyes of them both were opened" (Gn 3:7). They perceive themselves to be naked and sewed fig leaves together to cover themselves. A literal interpretation of this sentence would compel us to believe that Adam and Eve had walked around up to that point with their eyes closed. A real interpretation allows us to believe that Adam and Eve's biological eyes were open all along, but that their mental vision, their perception, changed after they committed the first sin of humanity—they saw their nakedness differently. This interpretation fits with the context and carries much more meaning than the strictly literal interpretation that the immediate consequence of original sin was merely to alter the position of four eyelids.

IMMEDIATE FASHIONING

The Fourth Lateran and First Vatican Councils (1215 and 1869–1870, respectively) declared that God "immediately from the beginning of time fashioned each creature out of nothing, spiritual and corporeal, namely angelic and mundane; and then the human creation, common as it were, composed of both spirit and body."[7] Following the logic of this statement, we understand that the soul cannot be said to evolve materially, since only material things can undergo physical change and the soul is immaterial. But the statement leaves open the possibility—quite evident from evolutionary science—that the body can, does, and will evolve. The doctrine given above, however, clearly rejects the materialist interpretation of the theory of evolution, the idea that everything including the soul (or mind) of humans emerges from physical material.[8]

The Pontifical Biblical Commission affirmed that humans must be regarded as a "special creation by God." It is *de fide* dogma that the first man was created by God, and this question is outside the realm of science anyway. Regardless of any scientific discovery in the fossil record, genetics, or comparative anatomy, nothing can ever prove that man was not created by God. As Catholics, we hold this truth in faith, not just for humans but for all creatures, all things.

As I indicated before in chapter 3, Ludwig Ott's *Fundamentals of Catholic Dogma* is a good place to discover the historical development of doctrine. Ott noted that the biblical text does not exclude the theory of evolution because, regarding the "question as to the mode and manner of the formation of the human body," an interpretation divergent from the literal sense is permissible but only in limited ways.[9] We cannot deny that God created the first human immediately out of nothing and science does not contradict that dogma.[10] The word "immediately" does not necessarily refer to succession in time; it can refer to the relation of a person or thing to another. "Immediate" can mean that there was no intermediary or intervening member, medium, or agent in contact or direct personal relation.[11]

We also cannot deny that God "vivified" the first human body by "breathing into it a spiritual soul," which science cannot comment on.[12] That humans consist of a material body and a spiritual soul is also *de fide* dogma. Both the material and spiritual aspects are essential. Again, the Fourth Lateran Council defined this teaching of "the human creation, common as it were, composed of both spirit and body."[13] Every human person has an individual soul.

As to the origin of the human soul, different opinions have been advanced. Pope Pius XII's 1950 encyclical *Humani Generis* said that "the Catholic faith obliges us to hold that souls are immediately created by God."[14] Do human souls preexist the conception of the human body? Early Christian Fathers accepted that they do because Plato held that view, and many of them were Platonic scholars, but the

Synod of Constantinople (543) rejected that view because it implies the possibility that a fall from grace could occur before the human body exists.[15]

Some thought the human soul originates with conception and comes from the parents, particularly the semen of the father, but this idea was condemned by Pope Benedict XII and Pope Leo XIII as incompatible with the simplicity and spirituality of the soul.[16] The soul cannot come from corporeal matter; for the soul to be "created immediately by God," it must be created out of nothing. Most theologians take that to mean that each individual soul is created by God out of nothing at the moment of conception. This is not defined in scripture, but indirectly expressed: "And the dust return into its earth, from whence it was, and the spirit return to God, who gave it" (Eccl 12:7).

POLYGENISM OR MONOGENISM

In *Humani Generis*, Pope Pius XII wrote that the question of the origin of the human body is open to careful research by scientists and theologians. He says that "the Teaching Authority of the Church does not forbid that, in conformity with the present state of human sciences and sacred theology, research and discussions, on the part of men experienced in both fields, take place with regard to the doctrine of evolution, in as far as it inquires into the origin of the human body as coming from pre-existent and living matter—for the Catholic faith obliges us to hold that souls are immediately created by God."[17] According to Ott, the scripture that says "And the Lord God formed man out of the slime of the earth: and breathed into his face the breath of life, and man became a living soul" (Gn 2:7) does not exclude the theory of evolution, but neither should the faithful assume that scripture proves that the human body evolved either.[18] The full meaning of this scripture is still a mystery.

As Catholics, we maintain the unity of the whole human race. This is not a *de fide* dogma, but rather a necessary presupposition of the dogma of original sin and redemption.[19] Polygenism is the view that the different races of mankind arose independently of one another, and that seems to contradict the unity of the human race. Pope Pius XII addressed polygenism, holding that "it is in no way apparent how such an opinion can be reconciled with that which the sources of revealed truth and the documents of the Teaching Authority of the Church propose with regard to original sin, which proceeds from a sin actually committed by an individual Adam and which, through generation, is passed on to all and is in everyone as his own" (*Humani Generis*, 37).

Pope Pius XII certainly argued against polygenism, but when *Humani Generis* was issued—three years before James Watson and Francis Crick reported that they had determined the helical structure of DNA in 1953—the understanding of the role genetics plays in evolution was only starting to develop. Sixty years later, Darwinian evolution has been reinterpreted in terms of molecular genetics, and the biological mechanism of evolution is better understood. Current scientific evidence points to a first population of humans rather than a single man and woman.

Later in the twentieth century, Fr. Karl Rahner explained that he did not take Pius XII's definition as an infallible rejection of polygenism.[20] Rahner argued that by using the words "in no way apparent," the pope seemed to be saying, very subtly, that it is not *plainly seen* how multiple first parents can be reconciled with the dogma of original sin. Rahner argued that those words leave the door cracked open for further development, that Pius was not declaring polygenism to be outright impossible. Therefore, polygenism might be possible if deeper insight were to be found, a way to understand polygenism without contradicting the doctrines of the fall, original sin, and the unity of the human race. Then monogenism (the view that all humans descend from one single human pair of parents) would not have to be defended. Here is the full quote from *Humani Generis*:

> When, however, there is question of another conjectural opinion, namely polygenism, the children of the Church by no means enjoy such liberty. For the faithful cannot embrace that opinion which maintains that either after Adam there existed on this earth true men who did not take their origin through natural

generation from him as from the first parent of all, or that Adam represents a certain number of first parents. Now it is in no way apparent how such an opinion can be reconciled with that which the sources of revealed truth and the documents of the Teaching Authority of the Church propose with regard to original sin, which proceeds from a sin actually committed by an individual Adam and which, through generation, is passed on to all and is in everyone as his own. (*Humani Generis*, 37)

Today, theologians and Catholic biologists more and more agree that there is substance to Rahner's opinion. It is worth noting that documents since *Humani Generis*, such as Pope Paul VI's 1965 *Gaudium et Spes*, which addresses social evolution toward unity, and the *Catechism of the Catholic Church*, issued in 1992, do not mention monogenism or polygenism, quite possibly indicating that theological developments are moving away from these terms.

Did God miraculously create the adult man, body and soul, instantly out of nothing or out of slime? Did humanity begin with that kind of miracle? Possibly, but such an event is not an investigation for science, which can only measure the results of physical laws. Was the first man a new conception that occurred in a highly evolved female primate womb, a zygote infused with the first rational human soul made in the image and likeness of God? Was the first woman, likewise, at some point later conceived in another female primate's womb as a soul mate for the man? Were they both born and both raised by non-human primates? And did they then mate after the fall? Whom did their children mate with? There are theological opinions that Adam and Eve's children mated with siblings. But how would they know not to mate with the other animals that looked like them but did not have rational souls? It seems unthinkable to say that the second generation of humans mated with nonhumans. Or is it?

Is, as some theologians suggest, the story in Genesis to be taken less literally, as a reality, but not a literal reality? Will there be theological developments in the future that refer to the first species of true humans as the "first man"? Will it be understood that they as a population fell from grace? Will it be understood that the unity of the human race was preserved even if there were a number of lineages? We simply do not know at this point in history. This is a matter for the trained scientists and trained theologians who inform the Magisterium, and ultimately it is a decision for the Magisterium, which safeguards the truths of faith. There will not be any declarations as long as the understanding remains ambiguous.

St. Augustine in the fourth century showed an appreciation for scientific discovery, but he also thought that knowledge of the quantitative exactness of the natural world and cosmos could not help us much in understanding the biblical message. Nevertheless, Augustine rejected any biblical interpretation that denied or ignored the established conclusions of natural studies. He was explicit on this point:

> It is often the case that a non-Christian happens to know something with absolute certainty and through experimental evidence about the earth, sky, and other elements of this world, about the motion, rotation, and even about the size and distances of stars, about certain defects [eclipses] of the sun and moon, about the cycles of years and epochs, about the nature of animals, fruits, stones, and the like. It is, therefore, very deplorable and harmful, and to be avoided at any cost that he should hear a Christian to give, so to speak, a 'Christian account' of these topics in such a way that he could hardly hold his laughter on seeing, as the saying goes, the error rise sky-high.[21]

My interpretation of this quote is that we should have faith in Christ before we ever get to science. My interpretation is also that Augustine realized when statements in the Bible conflict with hypotheses on the workings of nature, and when reason and observation provide no clear solution and decisive evidence, nor does scripture seem to be explicitly literal, then the matter is open to further inquiry. Whenever scientific reasoning seemed to settle a matter, however, Augustine urged that scripture would have to be reinterpreted. When a matter could not be settled, he said that he had no time for questions that "require much subtle and laborious reasoning to perceive which is the actual case," because it is not needed by those whom he wished to instruct for their own salvation and for the benefit of the Church.[22] In other words, St. Augustine knew that salvation did not come from knowledge of the natural world.

For now, and possibly forever, we do not know the exact details relating to human origins—not scientifically, not theologically. In the entire scope of history, those primal events, which could have happened in a single day, were but a fraction of a blink on an evolutionary scale that deals with thousands and millions of years at a time. If the two stories can never be plainly woven together, the discrepancy may be in the gap where humans cannot measure, not unlike the inaccessibility of the quantum realm.

MICROEVOLUTION AND MACROEVOLUTION

One fact about evolution that many people fail to understand is that microevolution and macroevolution are the same process at the molecular level. Microevolution refers to short times and small changes, and macroevolution refers to longer times and larger changes. It is the same kind of understanding when we note the difference in a stream and a canyon, the same process of change over longer times. If you have ever seen a puppy, you have witnessed a single step in microevolution. If you have ever seen a dog bred to desired traits, you have witnessed the results of a longer evolution in a population, albeit an artificial one because selection of parents for each generation of offspring was imposed by breeders.[23] The situations in different environments in nature can also cause "selection."

One may ask, "I have no trouble with microevolution among species, but how can macroevolution, where one species arises from another, occur?"

Evolution happens because of changes in gene frequencies over time. Gene frequency refers to how often a particular gene (DNA, sequenced for a specific trait) appears in a population. Researchers can determine gene frequency using DNA sequencing techniques. Suppose a scientist discovers variants for a specific trait and calls them gene A, gene B, and gene C. Then she collects DNA from individuals in a population and finds that half of them have gene A, a quarter of them have gene B, and the last quarter have gene C. She has thus determined that the gene frequency is 50, 25, and 25 percent respectively. If she repeats this study over successive generations and finds that the frequency changes to 30, 30, and 40 percent, then she knows that evolution has occurred by the processes of "genetic drift."

Gene frequencies can remain constant for long periods of time, or they can change quickly in response to changes in the environment. Suppose the environment was depleted of a certain food that individuals with gene A needed to live long enough to reach the age for reproduction. Those individuals would not reproduce at the same rate as the others, and the frequency of gene A would decrease. In this case, genetic drift would have occurred because of natural selection.

The process is the same on both short and long timescales. An example of microevolution is a bacterium population in a laboratory where a mutation (a change) occurs that creates a gene that causes the individual bacteria to divide more rapidly. Macroevolution refers to the evolutionary process over longer times, during which more gene frequencies change, sometimes enough for speciation to occur—for one species to divide into two.

Is there more to the story? Of course there is more. The structure of DNA was not known in Charles Darwin's time, but later the theory was expanded with knowledge of genetics. Today researchers such as Dr. Martin Nowak, professor of Biology and Mathematics and director of the Program for Evolutionary Dynamics at Harvard University, and a Roman Catholic, study a mathematical basis for evolution beyond genetics. Nowak argues that cooperation, not competition, is needed between organisms to build the social organizations that help them survive and reproduce.[24] This is a vibrant area of research, and while there is not enough room in this book to devote to all the compelling research into the cooperative aspect of evolution between individuals and species, be assured that the story of evolution is itself evolving. Our understanding does not grow by disregarding all that has been learned. Knowledge grows by adding to existing scientific theories.

It is understandable that people of faith are sometimes unsure what to think about evolution. Evolution is a complex scientific topic. On the one hand, evolution is as simple as genetic changes accumulating over time. The changes in the genetic material of individuals (the DNA) are not visible outside of a laboratory, but the effects of these changes sometimes can be seen in living creatures, things such as physical traits of the body (eye color, petal color, fin size, tail length), reproductive ability, life span, and social behaviors. The science that observes and measures these changes in populations is a fact-based science. On the other hand, evolution is also a theory in that it is a framework, a model, for how the diversity of life happened, and not everything about it is yet understood, including all the details of how macroevolution occurs. Nonetheless, evolutionary theory is supported by evidence from different sources, which is the hallmark of a theory that has gained strong confidence.

THE EVIDENCE FOR EVOLUTION

The following is a brief sketch, but enough to point you in the right direction if you are interested in learning more. Evolution is about traits that are inheritable. Over time there is a change in frequency of traits in a population of living things. Scientists can measure these changes and frequencies. Darwin, in *The Origin of Species*, was concerned with how these physical changes happened. He theorized, as scientists are supposed to do, that the natural environments imposed conditions that caused some organisms to better survive or better reproduce, and thus those organisms' traits were passed to the next generation in greater numbers. This is what Darwin called "natural selection."[25] In his book, Darwin listed many examples of different ratios of traits passed from generation to generation among plants and animals.

Since Darwin's time—and thanks to the work of the Roman Catholic friar Gregor Mendel, who is considered the "father of genetics" and of James Watson and Francis Crick, who determined the helical structure of DNA—evidence for the mechanism of evolution has been provided. Mendel experimented on pea plants and found that there are two alleles (DNA codes for genes) that determine flower color—one that codes for purple flowers and one for white flowers. Therefore, if you know the plant's flower color, called a phenotype, you can know something about its genetic makeup, called the genotype.

Since Mendel's time, scientists have figured out how to measure gene frequencies from one generation to the next, so they can measure gene frequency changes in populations where different selective forces are active. If they study organisms, such as the fruit fly, that reproduce very fast and in large numbers, scientists can observe evolution happening by measuring changes in the DNA sequence over generations under specified conditions. These changes are the nuts and bolts of the basic scientific evidence for evolution.

Fr. Paulinus Forsthoefel, S.J., gave a summary of the evidence for evolution found in the fossil record and in comparative anatomy in a full chapter of his book *Religious Faith Meets Modern Science*.[26] Fr. Forsthoefel was a professor emeritus of biology at the University of Detroit, a priest who taught in secular institutions, and therefore a role model for navigating science in the light of faith. I will summarize the evidence he listed.

The most commonly cited evidence for evolution comes from the remains of living things found in the strata of the Earth. There are frozen bodies of ice-age mammoths preserved for thousands of years. Trails and burrows of smaller animals have been found preserved from millions of years ago on petrified ancient beaches.

Early life forms—single-celled bacteria and cyanobacteria lacking organized genetic material—have been found in rocks 3 billion years old. They appear to have multiplied by fission. Around 1.5 billion years ago, cellular organisms with genetic material organized into chromosomes appear in the fossil record; they are called eukaryotes. The fossil record shows that only single-celled organisms such as these lived during several hundred million years. Then multicellular organisms appeared some 700 million years ago. Inferred from the burrows they left, they were likely worm-shaped. One hundred million years later, the fossil record shows remains of more complex but still soft bodies, such as jellyfish, and then animals with some primitive skeletal framework. During the Cambrian period some 570 million years ago, an abundance of hard-bodied animals appeared in what is commonly called the Cambrian explosion. All of these animals were invertebrates. Some, such as the trilobites, lived for millions of years and went extinct. Others, such as brachiopods and mollusks, were the ancestors of animals still living today. The evolution of chordates (animals with spinal cords) is well documented in the fossil record. Jawless fish appeared some 500 million years ago, then fish with jaws, then fish with fins, then amphibians, then reptiles, then birds, and then mammals. Between some species, though not for all, fossils of transitional animals, such as the archaeopteryx—not quite reptile, not yet bird—have been found.[27]

The evolution of plants is also recorded in the Earth's strata. Unicellular algae appeared about 1.5 billion years ago. Simple vascular plants appeared about 400 million years ago; then mosses, horsetails, and ferns, which all reproduce by spores; and then seed-bearing plants. Angiosperms appeared about 225 to 180 million years ago, and they diversified to produce the flowering plants we know today.[28]

Comparative anatomy strengthens the evidence for evolution. Consider the forelimb. Scientists studying the similarity within the diversity of skeletal structures in reptiles, amphibians, birds, and mammals have hypothesized that a primitive vertebrate ancestor might have had an upper bone, the humerus; two lower limb bones, the radius and ulna; and a hand with carpal bones and metacarpals as digits. This forelimb could have evolved in different ways to produce different animals. In primates, it could have stayed basically the same, while in others it changed. This could be why in birds the first digit is smaller and supports some of the feathered section of the wing, the second and third digits extend out to support most of the feathers, and the fourth and fifth digits are gone. Bats have a first digit, but it is not situated to support feathers, while the other four all elongate to support feathers, even though bats are featherless. Horses do not have a first or fifth digit, the second and fourth are small splints, and the third metacarpal extends long, capped by the hoof on the distal phalanx. These are examples of how different vertebrate animals may have evolved to their changing environments.[29]

The geographical distribution of plants and animals is another type of evidence that evolution occurs, many examples of which were listed by Charles Darwin. The finches found on the Galapagos Islands are a popular example. They were much like species found nearby in South America, but the finches on the islands evolved into several species in different ecological niches among the islands. Darwin hypothesized that these species were the descendants of finches that blew over from the mainland on high winds. Another example is the diverse armadillo species of South America, which evolved over time in the same geographical place. In the strata of rock, there are fossils of a similar armored mammal that might have been the ancestor of all the modern species.[30]

Other cases of similarities between geographically divided species have been explained by continental drift. Over the eons, the plates that make up the Earth's crust separate when material beneath them surges up, then split at fracture zones, move apart, and collide with other plates. Geologists have concluded that South America, India, and Africa were connected about 200 million years ago, but moved apart. Similar plant and animal fossils have been found on the three continents. Continental drift explains why similarities in the fossil record can be found on these three different land masses.[31]

Another compelling but more complex set of evidence for evolution resides in the entire taxonomy of living things. The Swedish botanist Carl Linnaeus devised the system, using Latin for universality, in the eighteenth century, and it has been greatly expanded and refined since then. The hierarchy we all learn in grade school—kingdom, phylum, class, order, family, genus, species—classifies organisms based on physical characteristics they share. These characteristics are explained by heredity (inheritance of biological characteristics).

Heredity is passed on through genetic material, and taxonomy relies on this mechanism. Thus, the taxonomy system is based on evolution. Organisms that can breed and produce fertile offspring are considered to be of the same species. If they are similar but cannot be crossed, they are in the same genus; the classification of similarities and differences continues systematically all the way out to the kingdoms of *Animalia*, *Plantae*, *Fungi*, *Protista*, *Archaea* and *Archaeabacteria*, and *Bacteria* and *Eubacteria*.

Linnaeus classified organisms originally according to anatomy and breeding, but genetics has added more to the story. The more alike two organisms are, the more they are thought to share a common heredity. Organisms with like characteristics are grouped together. For example, the scientific classification given to the house cat is *Felis catus*. *Felis* is a genus of cats in the family *Felidae* and includes the closest relatives of the domestic cat. They are small felines that feed on rodents or other small animals. Genetic studies indicate they evolved around 10 million years ago. The classification of the bobcat is *Lynx rufus*. There are many cat species divided into fewer genera, but all of these belong to the family *Felidae*, the order *Carnivora*, the class *Mammalia*, the phylum *Chordata*, and the kingdom *Animalia*.

Genetics allows scientists to actually compare the DNA of different organisms. Consistent with the taxonomic system, common origins can be inferred from the degree of genetic relationship between two organisms. Close ancestors have similar or even identical genomes. Fr. Forsthoefel, whose summary I am reviewing here, made this critical statement: "In proportion as organisms are more and more distantly related, the structures of their DNA's will differ."[32] The word "proportion" is significant because it refers to the genetic molecular mechanism of evolution.

Plants and animals are very different kinds of living things, yet genetics reveal that plants and animals had a common ancestor long ago. Both plants and animals reproduce by passing on genetic material made of the same isomeric forms of the twenty amino acids that build all the proteins for life. Both plants and animals use adenosine triphosphate (ATP) for energy storage. Both plants and animals multiply their cells through cell division.

A brief review of DNA structure is useful. DNA is double-stranded; each strand is a strand of nucleotides. Nucleotides are made of the five-carbon sugar deoxyribose, one of four nitrogenous bases (adenine, guanine, thymine, cytosine), and a phosphate group. To form a single strand, the sugars bond to the phosphate groups. To form the double strand, the single strands connect by hydrogen bonds between the bases. The pairing of the bases on the strands is very specific. A nucleotide with adenine (A) will only hydrogen-bond to thymine (T) in the other strand. Nucleotides with guanine (G) will only bond to nucleotides with cytosine (C). Therefore, if the order of bases in one strand is ATTACG, the order in the other strand will be TAATGC.[33]

Further, the four bases form a code in triplets, meaning there are sixty-four possible combinations of three bases each. Sixty-one of the triplet of bases code for one of the twenty amino acids used by organisms to make proteins. A strand of DNA has coding and noncoding regions, and the other three of the triplet codes are stop signals in the process of bonding amino acids into proteins.[34]

As would be expected, organisms of the same species have close to the same sequence of triplet coding. A difference in heredity is reflected in a difference in coding sequences. The degree of difference in sequences is a measure of how much heredity differs. There are tests that can compare the DNA of different organisms and quantify how much their heredity differs. The long DNA double-stranded helices of each organism are fragmented into short segments of a few hundred nucleotides. Then the short segments are heated to 100 degrees Celsius, causing the double strands to dissociate (separate) into single strands (the hydrogen bonds break). If the temperature is lowered, the hydrogen bonds will reform according to the complementary base pairs. Therefore, it is possible to dissociate DNA from two different organisms and allow one strand from one organism and the other strand from the other organism to recombine. The amount of recombination measures how identical the two organisms are genetically.[35]

For example, the DNA from humans and from chimpanzees is very similar, almost identical. Recombination tests reveal over 98 percent recombination, a result possible only if the sequences of genes for humans and chimpanzees nearly match. This is why researchers conclude that humans and chimpanzees have a common ancestor. If their genetics match that closely, then they are related by evolutionary descent. By comparison, the DNA of humans and chickens shows only 10 percent recombination. This lower number of genetic similarity tells scientists that humans and chickens share a very remote evolutionary ancestor, perhaps from the reptiles, a conclusion that would fit with the fossil record evidence that reptiles gave rise to both birds and mammals millions of years ago.[36]

There are now banks of homologous recombination (genetic matching) data, not just for the DNA strands but also for the amino acid sequences in the proteins of different animals. Fr. Forsthoefel concludes that "the point should be emphasized that all these evidences have cumulative effect, viz., the various pieces of evidence reinforce each other and all point to a common natural explanation in evolution."[37] Scientifically, there is no other theory that comes close to explaining the diversity of life found on our planet. In the words of geneticist Dr. Theodosius Dobzhansky, who was Eastern Orthodox and whose famous phrase provided the title of his essay in *The American Biology Teacher* in 1973: "Nothing in biology makes sense except in the light of evolution."[38]

HUMAN EVOLUTION

As it relates to human ancestry and with molecular genetics studies in mind, let us now turn to paleoanthropology. Paleoanthropology weaves a story of human evolution beginning in Africa about 4 million years ago. Humans appear to have evolved from apelike creatures that evolved from creatures before them. The fossil record shows that our branch of the tree of life, so to speak, includes the apes, the chimpanzees, the Neanderthals, and us—all evolutionary cousins.

The evidence is, as just explained, in the DNA. Scientists sequenced DNA from humans, apes, and chimpanzees, and their analysis of the data shows that we all arose from a common apelike ancestor. DNA is like a molecular clock in that the number of amino acid differences in proteins between different lineages changes roughly linearly with time (proportionally). Scientists have found that chimps seem to be most like humans (98 percent DNA match). By comparing the genomes of chimps with the human genome and then comparing that 2 percent difference against the rate at which specific genetic substitutions are known to occur, scientists have calculated that the lineages of chimps and humans diverged about 5 to 7 million years ago.

Fossils have been found for a large number of hominin (human evolutionary group of) species. They are described on the Smithsonian National Museum of Natural History website (http://humanorigins. si.edu), which certainly does not render the information gospel truth, but does give weight to the notion that these are the serious and real findings and estimations of scientific discovery. The list of fossils in the human family tree is staggering. Wade through this information from the Smithsonian website to gain an appreciation for the developing story line:

The earliest humans and closest link to other primates lived in Africa. *Sahelanthropus tchadensis* lived 7 to 6 million years ago. *Orrorin tugenensis* also lived about 6 million years ago. *Ardipithecus kadabba* lived about 5.8 to 5.2 million years ago. *Ardipithecus ramidus* lived about 4.4 million years ago.

On another branch arose the *Australopithecus* group. *Australopithecus anamensis* lived about 4.2 to 3.9 million years ago. *Australopithecus afarensis* lived about 3.85 to 2.95 million years ago. *Australopithecus garhi* lived about 2.5 million years ago. *Australopithecus africanus* lived about 3.3 to 2.1 million years ago.

On another branch evolved the *Paranthropus* group. *Paranthropus aethiopicus* lived 2.7 to 2.3 million years ago. *Paranthropus robustus* lived about 1.8 to 1.2 million years ago. *Paranthropus boisei* lived about 2.3 to 1.2 million years ago.

And then the *Homo* genus emerged, the group whose members were the first to expand beyond Africa. *Homo rudolfensis* lived about 1.9 to 1.8 million years ago. *Homo habilis* lived about 2.4 to 1.4 million years ago. *Homo erectus* lived about 1.89 million to 143,000 years ago; fossils were discovered in Java and China. *Homo heidelbergensis* lived about 700,000 to 200,000 years ago; fossils were discovered in Germany. *Homo floresiensis* lived about 95,000 to 17,000 years ago; fossils were found in Indonesia. And our friend *Homo neanderthalensis* lived about 200,000 to 40,000 years ago; fossils found in Germany, Belgium, and Gibraltar. Neanderthals made a diverse set of sophisticated tools, controlled fire, built houses, wore clothes, hunted large animals, ate plants, and made ornamental objects. There is evidence that they buried their dead and decorated graves, and that is why there is a good fossil record for this species.

Last, of course, came *Homo sapiens*, or "wise man," the hominin species that is modern man. *Homo sapiens* first appears in the fossil record in Africa during a period of climate change about 200,000 years ago. Both *Homo neanderthalensis* and *Homo sapiens* moved out of Africa. *Homo neanderthalensis* settled in Europe and Central Asia, and *Homo sapiens* eventually spread to the whole world. *Homo neanderthalensis* and *Homo sapiens* coexisted until the former went extinct about 39,000 to 41,000 years ago.[39] *Homo sapiens* is the only surviving hominin species.

In 1987, the journal *Nature* published the results from a worldwide survey of human mitochondrial DNA conducted by researchers in the Department of Biochemistry at the University of California, Berkeley. The researchers used genetic molecular clocks and showed that "all mitochondrial DNAs stem from one woman" who lived about 200,000 years ago in Africa.[40] The "one woman" quickly became known as Mitochondrial Eve, but these results do not suggest that there was only one woman alive at the time. Rather they suggest that she was one of many women of her time in a "genetic bottleneck," or a time when there was a small population. There are theories the size of the population was around 10,000 individuals.[41]

However, these population estimates come from computer simulations and probability models that extend assumptions about how many reproducing females might have lived and how many might have generated a persisting female line.[42] It should be noted that the models do not rule out a smaller population.[43]

The genetic inheritance for an offspring comes from both parents, and it is found in the nuclei of the egg and sperm cells. The DNA from the mother and father combine in the nucleus of the zygote, much as described in the discussion of recombination tests in the last section. DNA is also found in other parts of our cells. In the cytoplasm, there are organelles called mitochondria that provide ATP for energy in the cell. Mitochondria also contain DNA, but this DNA is transmitted to the offspring only from the mother. We all have four great-grand-mothers, but our mother's mother's mother (only one of the four) is the sole source of our mitochondrial DNA, even though the other three great-grandmothers and all four great-grandfathers contrib-uted genetic material. Thus, the claim that "all mitochondrial DNAs stem from one woman" that lived about 200,000 years ago in Africa is indeed remarkable, but the claim does not support a monogenetic origin of humankind, such as the biblical Eve.

Similar genetic studies regarding a Y-chromosome Adam were reported in 1995, also in the journal *Nature*.[44] The male-specific por-tion of the Y chromosome is useful for estimating when and where a common male ancestor existed.[45] The *Nature* article proposed that he lived about 188,000 years ago.[46] Like the mitochondrial DNA studies, the Y-chromosome studies suggest a human population size of about 10,000 in sub-Saharan Africa.[47] After 1995, further studies moved the time of the most recent common male ancestor up to about 140,000 years ago, which means that Mitochondrial Eve and Y-chromosome Adam would not have lived in the same time period. However, in 2013, a team at the University of Sassari in Italy studied the Y chro-mosomes of 1,200 men from the island of Sardinia and reported that those findings recalibrate the molecular clock, pushing Y-chromosome Adam back again to 180,000 to 200,000 years ago.[48] It is important to remember that these studies are ongoing.

In 2013, the Pontifical Academy of Sciences hosted a working group on "Neurosciences and the Human Person: New Perspectives on Human Activities." Because the topics are related, Dr. Yves Coppens presented a paper on "Hominid Evolution and the Emergence of the Genus *Homo*."[49] Dr. Coppens is an anthropologist who studies hominids (primates of the zoological family Hominidae including the great apes, their extinct relatives, and humans) and who was the director of the expedition to Hadar, Ethiopia, in 1974 that discovered AL 288-1, a group of several hundred pieces of bone constituting about 40 percent of the skeleton of a female *Australopithecus afarensis* popularly known as "Lucy." Dr. Coppens was named an ordinary member of the Pontifical Academy of Sciences by Pope Francis in 2014. In his paper, he referred to "Man" as a species. He began his paper by jovially stating the following about Man: "Let us remember, for the pleasure, that Man is a living being, an eucaryot, a metazoaires, a chordate, a vertebrate, a gnathostom, a sarcopterygian, a tetrapod, an amniot, a synapsid, a mammal, a primate, an Haplorhinian, a Simiiform, a Catarrhinian, an Hominoidea, an Hominidae, an Homininae and that life, on earth, is around 4 billion years old, metazoaires, 2 billion years old, vertebrates, 535 million years old, gnathostoms, 420 million years old, mammals, 230 million years old, Primates, 70 million years old, Hominoidea, 50 million years old, Hominidae, 10 million years old."[50]

His purpose was to convey the "state of the art" in paleoanthropology. He recounted the evidence for early prehumans, classic prehumans, late prehumans, early humans, classic humans, and late humans, and traced how each lineage evolved to their environment and spread out across a larger and larger territory, all becoming extinct except the population of *Homo sapiens sapiens* (modern humans), which moved to Europe 50,000 years ago and spread throughout the world, some of them still living among members of other species of the genus *Homo* who had not yet gone extinct. Since 10,000 years ago, there has been only one species and one subspecies, and that is our own.[51] He suggested that there will be no more new human subspecies on Earth because we have populated the whole planet, leaving no possibility for any group to be isolated enough for genetic drift to occur.

SORTING IT OUT

Back to the young man from the dinner party. Armed with this knowledge of the theological development of doctrine and of scientific progress, our stumped young man is better prepared to discuss evolution with his son. What does a parent say to a child about evolution? I think evolution is one of the hardest issues to discuss with children, but it can also be one of the most educational. I teach my children about the reality of Adam and Eve and the fall. I teach them, according to the *Catechism*, about original sin, the sacraments, and grace. I also teach them about dinosaurs, fossils, taxonomy, genetics, and yes, evolution. When they have questions about what the actual first human pair and subsequent generations were exactly like in time and space, I use that as an opportunity to begin to teach them the things I cover in this book. It is good to teach children that we do not have all the answers. It is good to teach them how to dive responsibly into the mystery of hard questions. It is good to teach them to think systematically by learning the difficult details so they can situate large amounts of information into a whole picture.

This is how I think about Genesis and the story of Adam and Eve.

It is like looking at a flower, symmetrical, mysterious, and beautiful. We see the flower and its glory, but we cannot see the flower down to every molecule, atom, and subatomic particle. That limitation is a fact of being human, a limitation that goes right along with our mental freedom to not only see with our eyes but to form abstractions in our minds. We can spend our whole lives pursuing knowledge and cheering on others for their discoveries. It means we can see more in the flower than what is literally visible to our eyes because we see with our scientific knowledge as well as with our senses. We can infer a reality that is beyond what is right in front of us.

Genesis is like this too. We read it, perfect beyond the literal, mysterious, and beautiful. We may assume that Adam and Eve, the first units of humanity, existed and began to live in a place and time because we have faith in divine revelation. But science, a magnificent feat of human intelligence for sure, is unable to find an Adam and an Eve.

Christians infer a reality that is beyond what is literal. We see more of what is really there.

What about the young father's conversation with the talkative evolutionary biologist? What he did was right. He listened and thought about what the other person was communicating. He respected the other man's opinion and expertise because the other man, as a working scientist, was sincerely trying to deepen our collective understanding. If we are confident in our faith and versed on what the Church teaches, we are prepared to listen to what someone outside the Church has to say. That does not mean we have to agree, but we can listen and strive to communicate in return.

A lot of people probably view the evolution question as divisive, but if you step back and look at what has happened since Darwin's time, you will see that evolution has actually united us. The Church accepts evolution so long as it remains understood as a process instituted by God, like everything else science studies. Atheists accept evolution, though they tend to assume that reality is restricted to what can be measured. We can all talk about the implications of evolution together.

What are the implications if Neanderthals and humans mated, as scientific evidence suggests they did? Were their offspring human beings? Were Neanderthals human beings with rational souls? Some scientists believe that they, and even *Homo erectus* before them, were intelligent and thus were human. If they were, is there anything we can learn from exploring what science suggests? Does it in any way shed more light on the meaning of being human? If we evolved, then in what ways are we still evolving? Can we guide our own evolution?

These questions are important and have a connection to our future. What if humans are ever cloned in laboratories against the advice of the Church? What if human-animal hybrids are ever cloned, also against the advice of the Church? Would those beings be human beings? What would be our obligations to them? What if human bodies are ever replaced with mostly robotic parts? What if it is ever claimed that our brains can be uploaded into computers, as some futurists predict? What if, as the inventor and futurist Ray Kurzweil predicts, there is a technological singularity in the year 2045 when computer intelligence, nanotechnology, and genetic alteration irreversibly transform people?[52]

The scientific conclusions thus far regarding human evolution are noteworthy. Since about 10,000 years ago, there has only been one species and one subspecies of *Homo sapiens*, and that is our own. Genetic studies indicate that all human females alive today are descendants of one *Homo sapiens* woman who lived about 200,000 years ago in Africa. Likewise, data points to a common male ancestor who lived about 200,000 years ago.

These estimates are not firm. Both Mitochondrial Eve and Y-chromosome Adam appear to come from separate populations of about 10,000 people. But remember, evolutionary science cannot get much narrower than this so far back in time. We should explore the science in the confidence of our faith and see what it has to show us.

CHAPTER 10

WHEN DOES A HUMAN LIFE BEGIN?

THE LOGIC OF LIFE

Some say the most intense intersection of faith and science lies in the realm of evolution, quantum mechanics, or cosmology. I say it lies in the quiet darkness of a mother's womb, where two cells merge to become one living human organism. Life itself is a mystery. We all begin life somewhat like Adam and Eve did—as bodies no other human knows about in our first moments of existence, invisible to the human record. By the time anyone knows about a new human life, it has already crossed the boundary from cell to organism, from a physical thing to a being, from science to faith.

Until now in this book, I have mostly approached life from the standpoint of physics and chemistry—which are indifferent to life—explaining that living things are physically composed of atoms and that life evolved from particles. But life is more than matter, as we well know because we see matter in its proper place in the system of wills. We need to discuss human life and that annoying question posed by people who know what they want the answer to be before they ask it: When does human life begin?

In biology textbooks, it is accepted and taught that living things reproduce because the production of offspring is basic to the continuance of any species. Evolutionary theory is foundational to biology because it is based on reproduction. Living things transmit their hereditary information from one generation to the next, and that transmission is based on the simple, singular fact that individual lives actually do begin.

In the process of mammalian reproduction, scientists likewise accept and teach that the sperm and the egg are single-cell gametes (the reproductive cells) produced by meiosis in the male and female parents. Each gamete contains half the genetic information needed for the formation of a new complete individual. The sperm fertilizes the egg cell, the genetic material combines, and a zygote cell forms. Then the zygote grows into an embryo and implants in the uterus of the mother and continues growing. It is agreed that fertilization is the process that marks the change from two gamete cells to a new individual organism.

Although the details at the molecular level of fertilization are complex, the reasoning really is that simple. It is common sense to take the uniting of the mother's and father's gamete cells into a new organism as the beginning of a new human life. But abortion advocates notoriously introduce subterfuge by opening up settled questions for debate.

Notice:

No one debates when an individual spider's life begins.

No one debates when an individual puppy's life begins.

No one debates when an individual chimp's life begins.

Without exception, the only beings subjected to such strange scrutiny about the beginning of their existence are unwanted human children.

Just as no one debates that the emergence of a new individual organism of any other species that reproduces this way is the beginning of the organism's life, no one debates when an individual *wanted* human child's life begins either. It is common sense to take fertilization as the beginning of the existence of a new human child. Human parents also do not go to labs to have their children tested to ensure that their offspring are not some other primate or other animal, for they know, as any reasonable person ought to know, that human parents do not beget arachnid, canine, or chimp offspring.

There are various other beginnings proposed for the life of an unwanted human child. One proposed beginning is gastrulation.

Gastrulation is the phase in embryonic development when the single-layer blastula folds and grows into a three-layered structure made up of the ectoderm, mesoderm, and endoderm. The cells in these layers become specific tissues and organs. Gastrulation occurs about two weeks after fertilization; the process of "twinning," by which a single zygote becomes two, is thought to occur before gastrulation if it is going to occur. The "twinning argument" against fertilization as the beginning of a new human child's life states that a zygote is not a living human organism because a zygote can become two living organisms. Therefore, according to that argument, the embryo (the multicellular human in the earliest stages of development) before gastrulation cannot be considered an individual human.

However, the timing of the twinning process is debated. In 2013, Dr. Gonzalo Herranz from the University of Navarre in Spain published a paper in the journal *Zygote* titled "The Timing of Monozygotic Twinning: A Criticism of the Common Model," in which he argues that monozygotic twinning is part of the fertilization process itself.[1] He explains that the first zygotic division that occurs after fertilization would produce not two blastomeres, but twin zygotes. If a zygote becomes twins during fertilization and the first cell division, then twinning is not a postfertilization event.

Another proposed marker of the beginning of individual unwanted human life is the detection of brain waves sometime around the eighth week of gestation. In 1985, Dr. John M. Goldenring at the New York Medical College argued in the *Journal of Medical Ethics* that the human embryo is not a "human being" until the organism has a "functioning brain."[2] He calls this the "brain-life theory," claiming symmetry with the determination of brain death as the cessation of brain waves measured by electroencephalograph (EEG). In this symmetrical view of humanness, "whenever a functioning brain is present, a human being is present." Conveniently, this view would mean that abortion before eight weeks gestation kills "potential human life" and not actual human life.

Furthermore, he argues, this view would remove ethical concerns with growing fetuses via in vitro fertilization for research or using aborted fetuses for research, provided they were under eight weeks of gestational age. The brain-life theory would also mean that contraception would not cause an abortion even if it prevented a living embryo from implanting in the uterine lining. Not surprisingly, supporters of the brain-life theory see it as a legitimate compromise between pro-abortion and anti-abortion advocates. They think that if they can convince people that human organisms in the earliest stages of development are not human beings, then killing them is not abortion.

Goldenring concludes that the brain-life theory would spare women from needing to "bury their menstrual flow with due religious ceremony on the chance that a spontaneous abortion has occurred."[3] He is referring to all the fertilized eggs who do not survive to birth. Going back as far as the 1970s, studies estimate that between 30 and 70 percent of zygotes do not survive to implantation and/or birth. Those high estimates mean that many, if not most, zygotes and embryos die naturally. Hence, if life begins at fertilization, it would follow that many normal menses carry bodies of dead children. If women truly believe that life begins at fertilization, then according to Goldenring, those women should be performing monthly religious ceremonies to bury the blood from their menstrual cycles on the chance that it contains a dead child. He concludes that since no civil society advocates this behavior, which is akin to ancient superstition, women should accept the brain-life theory.

My opinion as a Catholic woman is that the above remarks were not directed at women who use birth control but at us rebels who dare to embrace the Church's teaching about human life and motherhood. Plus, the argument presupposes that women are incapable of knowing much about their own bodies. My reasoning goes like this: if we see children as gifts, then we see our fertility as a gift. And if we see our fertility as a gift, then we ought to strive to understand our bodies. If we understand our bodies, then we know its cycles. If we know its cycles, then we have the best chance of knowing—even in the earliest days—when we are pregnant. Who do you think teaches this reasoning and knowledge to women? The Catholic Church does. Doctors ought to tell women the same, but it is hard to find any who do. There

are no ancient superstitions there, just biologically accurate information for women.

The scientist in me prefers to deal with the science strictly within
the limits of the discipline of biology, and within those boundaries we
should not treat a human organism *scientifically* any differently from
any other organism. If two gametes combine and the organism they
form is living, then for all we can conclude, as we conclude with any
other organism, the offspring is a living organism of its species. If most
of them die before birth, that death changes nothing about the fact
that they were living organisms of their species before death. If twins
form, then twins form. That is a process that ultimately we can know
about only after it occurs.

CROSSING THE BOUNDARIES OF SCIENCE

Problems arise when scientists playing ethicists try to discuss "life" as
"humanness" or "human being" or "personhood." Those words are outside the domain of science; to use them is to invoke a definition that is
beyond biology. Science, remember, does not declare what life is. Biology did not invent life. Biology studies, characterizes, and categorizes
living things based on observation.

In 2011, I noticed a peculiar consequence of the equivocation surrounding the terms "life" and "being" and "personhood." In the eighth
edition (as in the later ninth and tenth editions) of his college textbook *Developmental Biology*, Prof. Scott F. Gilbert has a chapter called
"Fertilization: Beginning a New Organism."[4] For the eighth edition
there was also supplemental material online for this chapter that contained an accompanying essay, written by Gilbert, titled "When Does
Human Life Begin?"

The essay opened with this statement: "The question of when
a human life begins is a profoundly intricate one, with widespread
implications, ranging from abortion rights to stem cell research and
beyond. A key point in the debate rests on the way in which we choose
to define the concepts of humanity, life and human life. What does it
mean to be alive? What does it mean to be human? Is a zygote or an
embryo alive? Is a zygote or an embryo a human being?"[5]

Why, I wondered, *is a developmental biologist asking whether or not a new organism is alive just because it is human?* Would not a living human embryo be alive just as any other living embryo? For the tenth edition, there is a new online companion essay with a different title, "When Does Human Personhood Begin?"[6] The word "life" in the title has been changed to "personhood," and the new essay focuses on whether fertilization, gastrulation, EEG activity, viability, or birth marks the beginning of *personhood*.

The words are still getting mixed up. Gilbert gave a lecture in 2010 to the American Reproductive Health Professional Society titled "When Does Human Life Begin?" In that talk, he reviewed the developmental markers listed above as proposed beginnings of "personhood," emphasizing how scientists do not know when personhood begins. But then he stated: "So one of the questions one has to ask is: Why does the public even think that life can begin at fertilization?"[7]

Why? I submit that people think life begins at fertilization for the same reason Gilbert called a chapter of his textbook "Fertilization: Beginning a New Organism." It is obvious.

To be fair, the ethical discussion is focused on "personhood" and not "human organism," but this is precisely why we need to be clear about the different questions science and faith can answer. "Personhood" is not a scientific question (as discussed in chapter 6). Just as the explanation of the absolute beginning of the universe does not belong to cosmology, the explanation of free will does not belong to quantum mechanics, and the full explanation of human existence does not belong to evolution, the understanding of personhood does not belong to developmental biology. The fullest answer, for all of these big questions, *requires faith as well as reason.*

FINDING CLARITY IN FAITH

Science did not open my eyes to the fuller view of motherhood and childhood; faith did. I remember the three words that changed my mind: *Children are gifts.* The first time I opened the *Catechism of the Catholic Church*, the first line I read was, "A child is not something *owed* to one but is a *gift*" (*CCC*, 2378). It is my opinion now that the word *gift* is the only definition of children that makes sense. Children are gifts; they are beings bestowed to parents. Since they are gifts from God, they are good. Like any gift, maybe they are surprises and maybe they are not fully appreciated at the moment of bestowing, but if parents freely give love unconditionally, they will see the immeasurable value in the gift of a child.

I think Catholics need to stop invoking only science as proof that human life begins at conception. Science cannot declare that full truth. How can we show others the beauty of the unity of faith and science if we leave out faith? Our faith tells us that if there is a human body, there is a human soul. Scientifically, we are not sure when during fertilization a new human comes into being, but we are sure that a healthy human zygote is a healthy human body at its early developmental stage. Together these truths inform us that those humans are worthy of life and protection.

Perhaps there are times when two gametes combine genetically and do not constitute a human organism, and thus the nonorganism never lives or grows. Perhaps there are zygotes that later become twins. Perhaps there have been more humans who died before implantation than survived to birth, and perhaps heaven is full of these souls. The fact is that we do not know. There are no little Martians hiding in women's wombs reporting out to the researchers exactly what happens in there. The best person to know what goes on in a woman's womb is the woman herself, and she can know a lot if she is paying attention.

By my figuring, 42 percent of my fertilized eggs miscarried, so I do not find the 30 to 70 percent estimate shocking. The five times I miscarried, I knew I was pregnant on the earliest possible day. If I had not been following the teaching of natural family planning, I might not have known when my own children came into existence. Rather than adopting the suggestion of Goldenring to have monthly funerals in ignorance, I have sought to know about my children. Maybe those pregnancies were not from living embryos but were "chemical" pregnancies, as one doctor put it, or maybe our family really did experience a few weeks with a little family member briefly alive in my womb. I am satisfied knowing that to the best of my ability I have loved my children unconditionally. Truth may demand more of us, but truth brings sanity.

Even if people do not understand it, we need to keep proclaiming that "life begins at conception." "Conception" is a beautiful word fitting for the initiation of human life. Its etymon is, of course, the classical Latin word *conception-*, *conceptio*, meaning the action or fact of conceiving in the womb. In postclassical Latin, it also meant comprehension, as in to know—not only to hold in your hands but to behold in your heart and mind. The word "conception" means literally "the action of first coming into being."[8] Putting the two meanings together, to say "life begins at conception" is to say that life begins when we know it comes into being.

That view turns the arguments around. We do not place ourselves before fertilization as judges determining when life will occur or not occur depending on our desires. We place ourselves, as any good scientist ought to, as observers seeking to understand (literally, to "stand under") the truth that life exists once it exists. We are observers, not dictators commanding fantasies. The proclamation that life begins at conception is a tautological statement. That truth belongs to anyone who will accept it. As Mother Mary taught us, life is a *fiat*.

It is most satisfying to remember a quote from Flannery O'Connor in *The Habit of Being*: "I think that when I know what the laws of the flesh and the physical really are, then I will know what God is. We know them as we see them, not as God sees them. For me it is the virgin birth, the Incarnation, the resurrection which are the true laws of the flesh and the physical. Death, decay, destruction are the suspension of those laws. I am always astonished at the emphasis that the Church puts on the body. . . . The resurrection of Christ seems the high point in the law of nature."[9]

CONCLUSION

SUMMARIZING THE THREES

I wove three stories into this book. Regarding *my experiences*, I told the story about my encounter with the chasm between what nature does and what we do in laboratories to make these points: (1) Science and scientists do not have all the answers because we are only human and acquire knowledge in steps. (2) Every scientist faces what I called "the chasm," the big truth beyond science that insists on the question, "Where did all this come from?" (3) Every human is a wayfarer, a gravity-bound creature working through life.

Regarding *faith*, I told the story about entertaining our nonreligious dinner guests to make what I think is the single most important point of this book. If (1) faith illuminates the encounter with science, then (2) faith comes first. (3) Never, ever upend that order. We evangelize, even within the scope of scientific inquiry, by radiating the light out to those who have not accepted the gift of faith. People may argue this point by saying that there is no hierarchy between faith and reason, that faith and reason are to be used equally in the search for truth. I am not saying otherwise, but as it relates to *scientific* reason, and all the inductive evidence it can provide, it must remain subordinate to faith because science alone can never prove the truths we hold in faith. Science can give us deeper understanding and insight. Science can inspire us to express awe and wonder.

Regarding *science*, I told the story of the atom to make the point that (1) something as fundamental to science as the atom, well understood down to unimaginable particle masses and forces, is still developing and always will be. There is order and design in the atom, in the history of the atoms, in the relation of atoms to each other, in the prescribed laws that govern their actions. (2) It is a testament to our rationality that humans have discovered all of these particles and interactions, and it is a fact of our humanity that our knowledge will forever remain partial, but (3) if we see science in the light of faith, then we take the richest, most reasonable, and vastly more exciting approach to scientific enterprise, respecting nature as a part of a bigger systematic reality.

I offered three analogies that I have found helpful when communicating about faith and science. Faith is not merely trying to hang on to the Battleship of Scientism. Rather, science emerged from faith in an ordered and predictable universe. The relationship, like that between Susie and Johnny, is best understood in its full history and not only from the chatter of the current day. The relationship between faith and science is more than a friendship, though. It is a unity of different manifestations of reality. The relationship between faith and science is best understood in the way we bless our meals. Our meals made of atoms are science viewed as gifts from God.

I gave three steps for navigating science in the light of faith. (1) Know what the Church teaches. (2) Begin to learn the science. (3) Sort out the system of wills. This phrase "system of wills" is my own, but used as a placeholder to explain St. Thomas Aquinas's teaching along with a metaphor borrowed from C. S. Lewis that nature is a medium (hostess) in which we act. God created prescriptive laws; we formulate descriptive models of those laws to the best of our ability at each moment in history. While a physical scientist may need to view the world as if it had no free agents, a scientist also knows this is an assumption made for the sake of defining a system in which he can say "all other things being equal." Free agents with free will and intellect, made in the image and likeness of God, can move matter too. We are part of the greater system of wills. When God intervenes to move matter, he does not break the laws of nature. Rather, his will represents the supreme law.

Regarding the questions posed to faith by physics, I gave these answers, but I also framed many of them as my opinion. I did this for a reason—to demonstrate to the reader how to navigate the questions as a person. You know where I stand, but I expect some of my views to be debated by those who disagree. I expect my opinions to mature thanks to those who will pose challenges and questions. This is another enjoyable aspect of being human.

Last, let us review the questions and answers. Does the Big Bang prove God? I said that it does, but only in the same way a sunset does. Physical science can provide inductive evidence to corroborate and complement a deductive claim that God created the universe. As Christians, we view everything as created by God, ubiquitously, just as early Christians and ancient Hebrews did, many of whom were martyrs. Is the atomic world the real world? This may seem like an obvious answer, but it set the stage for a discussion about quantum mechanics. The atomic world is real but invisible, and dazzling information about it continues to unfold in our time thanks to ongoing research. Does quantum mechanics explain free will? In the sense that the behavior of matter follows *prescriptive* laws of nature, we can call it intransitively deterministic. In the sense that our models are *descriptive* and cannot fully describe all motion of particles moving in systems, matter is transitively indeterminate and probabilistic. Quantum mechanics cannot explain free will because free will is not a subject of particle physics.

With those distinctions about physics in place, we were then ready to enter the biological questions. Did we evolve from atoms? Yes, not only did we evolve from atoms, we evolved from the beginning since our bodies are made up of matter. However, we are not only bodies, we are also human souls, so evolution can never fully account for the diversity of life and our existence as humans. Are creationism and intelligent design correct? I say no. Creationists seem to reject science because they fear it can prove faith wrong. Intelligent design theorists take too narrow a view of what is and what is intelligently designed; they rely on science to tell us what faith already does. Can a Christian accept the theory of evolution? Yes, a Christian can accept and follow the scientific developments, and a Christian can still believe that God miraculously created Adam and Eve, which science can never find. When does a human life begin? We are not sure, but we know that a healthy human zygote is a healthy, living, growing human being. Biology does not declare or define life. Biology observes life after it has begun. When we say life begins at conception, we uphold the simplest unity of faith and science.

These are things I hope you remember.

BEYOND SCIENCE

The book now ends by pointing beyond the particles because our Catholic faith begins and ends with miracles. The Catholic Church stands out in the world as supernatural, at home in but not of this world. We, human persons, likewise stand out beyond nature. I am most fond of this scripture passage, one that Fr. Jaki often cited: in the Gospel of Mark, when Christ calls the multitude together with his disciples, he says to them, "For what shall it profit a man, if he gain the whole world, and suffer the loss of his soul?" (Mk 8:36). Science may point to heaven, but science will not get us there.

Seeing science in the light of faith means we stand glorious with faith in the Holy Trinity, a beginning in time, angels, the soul, personhood, the annunciation, the visitation, the Incarnation, the Baptism, the water turned into wine, the Beatitudes, the Transfiguration, the Eucharist, the Agony in the Garden, the Scourging at the Pillar, the Crown of Thorns, the Carrying of the Cross, the Crucifixion, the Resurrection, the Ascension of Christ, the Descent of the Holy Spirit, the assumption of Mary, and her Crowning as the Queen of Heaven and Earth.

None of these is a subject of physical science. Christianity is not a theory.

Francis Bacon may have been partially correct in saying that "the nature of every thing is best seen in its smallest portions," at least for those of us who cannot look at leaves or pizza without thinking about atoms. But if we stop there, reality falls mechanically flat, and we miss the total interlocking system of reality. Our actions as free agents change the course of nature as we play the song of human life on Earth. All the while, the particles in this medium respond according to the laws governing them. And the miracles of God crown the hymn of creation.

NOTES

1. A STORY ABOUT THE CHASM

1. Albert Einstein, *The World As I See It*, trans. Alan Harris (New York: Citadel Press/Carol Publishing Group), 28.

2. Jonathan Weiner, *The Next One Hundred Years: Shaping the Fate of Our Living Earth* (New York: Bantam Books, 1990).

3. Ibid., 26–38.

4. Ibid., 38.

5. Ibid., 26, quoting Francis Bacon, *The New Organon*.

6. K. Eric Drexler and Chris Peterson, *Unbounding the Future: The Nanotechnology Revolution* (New York: Quill, 1991).

7. Ibid., 185.

8. Steven W. Keller, Stacy A. Johnson (Trasancos), Elaine S. Brigham, Edward H. Yonemoto, and T. E. Mallouk, "Photoinduced Charge Separation in Multilayer Thin Films Grown by Sequential Adsorption of Polyelectrolytes," *Journal of the American Chemical Society* 117, no. 51 (1995): 12879–12880; T. E. Mallouk, S. W. Keller, C. M. Bell, H.-G. Hong, H.-N. Kim, Y. I. Kim, D. M. Kaschak, D. L. Feldheim, P. J. Ollivier, and S. A. Johnson (Trasancos), "Self-Assembly of Nanostructures from Inorganic Building Blocks," *Proceedings of the Robert A. Welch Conference on Chemical Research XXXIX Nanophase Chemistry* (1995): 123–137; S. W. Keller, S. A. Johnson (Trasancos), E. H. Yonemoto, E. S. Brigham, G. B. Saupe, and T. E. Mallouk, "Photochemically Induced Charge Separation in Electrostatically Constructed Organic Inorganic Multilayer Composites," in *Photochemistry and Radiation Chemistry: Complementary Methods for the Study of Electron Transfer*, Advanced Chemistry Series 254, ed. D. G. Nocera and J. S. Wishart (Washington, DC: American Chemical Society, 1998), 359–379; D. M. Kaschak, S. A. Johnson (Trasancos), C. C. Waraksa, J. Pogue, and T. E. Mallouk, "Artificial Photosynthesis in Lamellar Assemblies of Metal Poly(pyridyl) Complexes and Metalloporphyrins," *Coordination Chemistry Reviews*, 185–186 (1999): 403–416.

9. Keller et al., "Photoinduced Charge Separation," 12879–12880.

10. S. A. Johnson (Trasancos), E. S. Brigham, P. J. Ollivier, and T. E. Mallouk, "The Effect of Pore Topology on the Structure and Properties of Zeolite Polymer Replicas," *Chemistry of Materials* 9 (1997): 2448–2458. S. A. Johnson (Trasancos), D.

Khushalani, G. A. Ozin, T. E. Mallouk, and N. Coombs, "Polymer Mesofibres," *Journal of Materials Chemistry*, 8 (1998): 13–14. Stacy A. Johnson (Trasancos), Patricia J. Olliver, and Thomas E. Mallouk, "Ordered Mesoporous Polymers of Tunable Pore Size From Colloidal Silica Templates," *Science* 283, no. 5404 (1999): 963–965.

11. Donald Voet and Judith G. Voet, *Biochemistry* (New York: John Wiley and Sons, 1990), 16.

12. Jearl Walker, David Halliday, and Robert Resnick, *Fundamentals of Physics Extended*, 13th Edition (Hoboken, NJ: John Wiley and Sons, 2014), 1335.

2. ANALOGIES ABOUT HOW FAITH AND SCIENCE RELATE

1. *Oxford English Dictionary (OED) Online*, s.v. "science," accessed February 28, 2016, http://www.oed.com/view/Entry/172672.

2. Thomas Aquinas, *The Works of St. Thomas Aquinas*, Latin-English ed., trans. Laurence Shapcote, ed. John Mortensen and Enrique Alarcon, vol. 13, *Summa Theologiæ, Prima Pars, 1–49* (Lander, WY: The Aquinas Institute for the Study of Sacred Doctrine, 2012), 3 (I.1.1).

3. *OED Online*, s.v. "science."

4. *OED Online*, s.v. "trivium" and "quadrivium," accessed February 28, 2016, http://www.oed.com/view/Entry/20653 and http://www.oed.com/view/Entry/155752.

5. *OED Online*, s.v. "art," accessed February 28, 2016, http://www.oed.com/view/Entry/11125.

6. *OED Online*, s.v. "scientism," accessed February 28, 2016, http://www.oed.com/view/Entry/172696.

7. *OED Online*, s.v. "belief," accessed February 28, 2016, http://www.oed.com/view/Entry/17368.

8. René Descartes, *Discourse on the Method of Rightly Conducting the Reason, and Seeking Truth in the Sciences*, Part VI (Project Gutenberg, 2008), accessed December 5, 2015, http://www.gutenberg.org/files/59/59-h/59-h.htm#part6.

9. Francis Bacon, preface to *The New Organon or: True Directions Concerning the Interpretation of Nature*, in *Complete Works* (Minerva Classics, 2013), Kindle edition.

10. Christopher Baglow, *Faith, Science, and Reason: Theology on the Cutting Edge* (Mobile, AL: Midwest Theological Forum, 2012), 20.

3. NAVIGATING SCIENCE IN THE LIGHT OF FAITH

1. *OED Online*, s.v. "provision" and "provisional," accessed February 28, 2016, http://www.oed.com/view/Entry/153483 and http://www.oed.com/view/Entry/153485.

2. Thomas Aquinas, *De Ente et Essentia* [On Being and Essence], first line.

3. Paulinus F. Forsthoefel, *Religious Faith Meets Modern Science* (New York: Alba House, 1994), 126–127.

4. Heinrich Denzinger, *Enchiridion Symbolorum: Compendium of Creeds, Definitions, and Declarations on Matters of Faith and Morals*, Latin/English, 43rd ed., ed. Peter Hünermann (San Francisco: Ignatius Press, 2012), 8.

5. Ibid.

6. Ibid.

7. Ibid.

8. Ludwig Ott, *Fundamentals of Catholic Dogma*, ed. James Canon Bastible (Charlotte, NC: TAN Books, 1974); Heinrich Denzinger, *The Sources of Catholic Dogma*, trans. Roy J. Deferrari, in *Enchiridion Symbolorum*, 30th ed. (Fitzwilliam, NH: Loreto Publications, 1954).

9. St. Thérèse of Lisieux, *Histoire d'une Ame*, trans. John C. H. Wu, EWTN Library (1895), accessed December 5, 2015, https://www.ewtn.com/library/SPIRIT/SCI-LOVE.TXT.

10. John Paul II, "Letter of His Holiness John Paul II to Reverend George V. Coyne, SJ, Director Of The Vatican Observatory," Vatican, June 1, 1988.

11. Aquinas, *Works* 14:519 (*Summa Theologiæ* I.105.6).

12. Ibid.

13. Aquinas, Works 14:75 (*Summa Theologiae* I.58.3).

14. Ibid.

15. Aquinas, *Works* 14:75 (*Summa Theologiæ* I.59.2).

16. Aquinas, Works 14:75 (*Summa Theologiae*, I.58.3).

17. Ibid.

18. Aquinas, Works, 14:520 (*Summa Theologiae*, I.105.6).

19. Aquinas, Works 14:521 (*Summa Theologiae*, I.105.7).

20. C. S. Lewis, *Miracles: A Preliminary Study* (New York: Harper Collins, 2001 reprint), 94.

21. Ibid., 93.

22. Ibid.

23. Ibid., 95.

24. Aquinas, *Works* 14:521 (*Summa Theologiæ* I.105.7).

4. DOES THE BIG BANG PROVE GOD?

1. Georges Lemaître, "Expansion of the Universe: A Homogeneous Universe of Constant Mass and Increasing Radius Accounting for the Radial Velocity of Extra-galactic Nebulae," *Monthly Notices of the Royal Astronomical Society* 91 (1931): 483–490.

2. Georges Lemaître, "The Beginning of the World from the Point of View of Quantum Theory," *Nature* 127 (1931): 706.

3. Pius XII, "The Proofs for the Existence of God in the Light of Modern Natural Science," *Address to the Pontifical Academy of Sciences*, November 22, 1951, 44, https://www.ewtn.com/library/PAPALDOC/P12EXIST.HTM

4. Ibid., 51.

5. Rodney D. Holder and Simon Mitton, eds., *Georges Lemaître: Life, Science and Legacy*, (New York: Springer, 2012), 71–72.

6. Pius XII, *Acta apostolicae sedis*, Vol. 44 (Vatican City State: Tipografia Poliglotta Vaticana, 1952), 739.

7. Holder and Mitton, *Georges Lemaitre*, 72.

8. Pius XII, "The Proofs for the Existence of God in the Light of Modern Natural Science,"45.

9. Ron Cowen, "Telescope Captures View of Gravitational Waves," *Nature* 507, 281–283 (20 March 2014), accessed January 28, 2016, http://www.nature.com/news/telescope-captures-view-of-gravitational-waves-1.14876.

10. Leslie A. Wickman, "Does the Big Bang Breakthrough Offer Proof of God?" *CNN Belief Blog*, March 20, 2014, http://religion.blogs.cnn.com/2014/03/20/does-the-big-bang-breakthrough-offer-proof-of-god/.

11. Leslie A. Wickman, *God of the Big Bang: How Modern Science Affirms the Creator* (Brentwood, TN: Worthy Publishing, 2015), 6.

12. Ron Cowen, "Gravitational Waves Discovery Now Officially Dead," *Nature News*, January 30, 2015, http://www.nature.com/news/gravitational-waves-discovery-now-officially-dead-1.16830.

13. Adrian Cho, "Gravitational waves, Einstein's ripples in spacetime, spotted for first time," *Science News*, February 11, 2016, http://www.sciencemag.org/news/2016/02/gravitational-waves-einstein-s-ripples-spacetime-spotted-first-time.

14. LIGO Caltech, "Gravitational Waves Detected 100 Years After Einstein's Prediction," News Release, February 11, 2016, https://www.ligo.caltech.edu/news/ligo20160211.

15. Ibid.

16. Robert Spitzer, *New Proofs for the Existence of God: Contributions of Contemporary Physics and Philosophy* (Grand Rapids, MI: Eerdmans, 2010), 22.

17. Ibid., chap. 3–5.

18. Peter Hodgson, *Theology and Modern Physics* (Oxford: Ashgate, 2005), chap. 10.

19. Aquinas, *Works* 13:478 (*Summa Theologiæ* I.46.2).

20. International Theological Commission, "Communion and Stewardship: Human Persons Created in the Image of God"(Vatican City: Libreria Editrice Vaticana, 2004), 67, http://www.vatican.va/roman_curia/congregations/cfaith/cti_documents/rc_con_cfaith_doc_20040723_communion-stewardship_en.html.

21. *OED Online*, s.v. "ubiquitous" and "nullibiquitous," accessed April 2, 2016, http://www.oed.com/view/Entry/208516 and http://www.oed.com/view/Entry/261214.

22. Aquinas, *Works* 13:427 (*Summa Theologiæ* I.22.2).

23. "Previous Prize Winners," Templeton Prize website, accessed December 5, 2015, http://www.templetonprize.org/previouswinner.html.

24. Stacy Trasancos, *Science Was Born of Christianity: The Teaching of Fr. Stanley L. Jaki* (Titusville, FL: The Habitation of Chimham Publishing Company, 2014).

25. Stanley L. Jaki, *Science and Creation: From Eternal Cycles to an Oscillating Universe* (Edinburgh: Scottish Academic Press, 1986).

26. Trasancos, *Science Was Born of Christianity*, 41–85.

27. Jaki, *Science and Creation*, 6–7.

28. Stanley Jaki, *The Savior of Science* (Grand Rapids, MI: William B. Eerdmans Publishing Company, 2000), 26.

29. Alexander Roberts, Sir James Donaldson, Arthur Cleveland Coxe, editors, *Ante-Nicene Fathers Volume I: The Apostolic Fathers, Justin Martyr, Irenaeus* (New York: Charles Scribner's Sons, 1925), 169; quoted in Jaki, *Science and Creation*, 164.

30. Roberts, *Ante-Nicene Fathers Volume I*, 191; Jaki, *Science and Creation*, 165.

31. Alexander Roberts, Sir James Donaldson, Arthur Cleveland Coxe, eds., *Ante-Nicene Fathers Volume II: Fathers of the Second Century: Hermes, Tatian, Athenagoras, Theophilus, and Clement of Alexandria* (New York: Charles Scribner's Sons, 1925) 131; quoted in Jaki, Science and Creation, 164.

32. Roberts, *Ante-Nicene Fathers Volume II*, 136; Jaki, *Science and Creation*, 164.

33. Ibid.

34. Clement of Alexandria, trans. by G. W. Butterworth, *The Exhortation to the Greeks, The Riches of Man's Salvation, and the Fragment of an Address Entitled To the Newly Baptized* (London: William Heinemann, 1919), 153; quoted in Jaki, *Science and Creation*, 168.

35. Ibid.

36. Alexander Roberts, Sir James Donaldson, Arthur Cleveland Coxe, eds., *Ante-Nicene Fathers Volume IV: Tertullian, Part Fourth; Minucius Felix; Commodian; Origen, Part First and Second* (New York: Charles Scribner's Sons, 1925), Origen, *De Principiis*, Book II, chapter 3 "On the Beginning of the World, and Its Causes," 273.

37. Roberts, *Ante-Nicene Fathers Volume IV*, 273; quoted in Jaki, *Science and Creation*, 171.

38. Jaki, *Science and Creation*, 175.

5. IS THE ATOMIC WORLD THE REAL WORLD?

1. Theodore L. Brown, H. Eugene LeMay Jr., Bruce E. Bursten, Catherine J. Murphy, Patrick M. Woodward, and Matthew W. Stoltzfus, *Chemistry: The Central Science*, 13th ed. (Boston, MA: Pearson, 2015), 939.

2. Michael Wysession, David Frank, Sophia Yancopoulos, *Physical Science: Concepts in Action* (Upper Saddle River, NJ: Pearson Prentice Hall, 2006), 536–537.

3. *OED Online*, s.v. "quantum," accessed February 28, 2016, http://www.oed.com/view/Entry/155941.

4. Brown, et al., *Chemistry: The Central Science*, 216–217.

5. Ibid., 217–227.

6. Walker, Halliday, and Resnick, *Fundamentals of Physics*.

7. Ibid., 1336.

8. Ibid., 1336.

9. Ibid., 1338.

10. Ibid., 1347.

11. Ibid.

12. Ibid., 1350.

13. Ibid., 1351.

14. Ibid., 1344.

15. Ibid., 1339.

16. Ibid., 1354.

17. Ibid.

18. Denis Edwards, "Toward a Theology of Divine Action: William R. Stoeger, SJ, on the Laws of Nature," *Theological Studies* 76:3 (2015): 485–502.

6. DOES QUANTUM MECHANICS EXPLAIN FREE WILL?

1. Nigel Calder, *Einstein's Universe* (Avenel, NJ: Wings Books, 1982), 141.

2. Albert Einstein to Max Born, trans. Irene Born, *The Born–Einstein Letters: Correspondence between Albert Einstein and Max and Hedwig Born from 1916 to 1955 with Commentaries by Max Born* (London: Macmillan Press, 1971), 149.

3. *OED Online*, s.v. "determine," accessed February 28, 2016, http://www.oed.com/view/Entry/51244.

4. Stanley L. Jaki, *A Mind's Matter: An Intellectual Autobiography* (Grand Rapids, MI: William B. Eerdman's Publishing Company), 165.

5. Stanley L. Jaki, *Intelligent Design?* (Port Huron, MI: Real View Books, 2005), 5.

6. Hodgson, *Theology and Modern Physics*, 133.

7. I am grateful to my husband for this analogy, one he uses in the business world as well when people try to predict more than they can.

8. Ibid., 225.

9. Lemaître, "The Beginning of the World," 706.

10. Ibid., 706.

11. *OED Online*, s.v. "person," accessed February 28, 2016, http://www.oed.com/view/Entry/141476.

12. Aquinas, *Works* 13:307 (*Summa Theologiæ* I.29.1.1).

13. Ibid., 13:311 (*Summa Theologiæ* I.29.2).

14. Ibid., 13:319 (*Summa Theologiæ* I.30.2).

15. Dan Barker, "What Is a Freethinker?" *Freedom from Religion Foundation* website, FAQs, accessed December 5, 2015, http://ffrf.org/faq/feeds/item/18391-what-is-a-freethinker.

16. Sam Harris, *Free Will* (New York: Free Press, 2012), 5.

17. Victor Stenger, "Free Will Is an Illusion," *Huffington Post Science*, June 1, 2012, http://www.huffingtonpost.com/victor-stenger/free-will-is-an-illusion_b_1562533.html.

18. Stephen Hawking and Leonard Mlodinow, *The Grand Design* (New York: Bantam, 2010), 32.

19. Thomas Aquinas, *Summa Contra Gentiles*, chap. 13.7, accessed December 5, 2015, http://dhspriory.org/thomas/ContraGentiles1.htm.

7. DID WE EVOLVE FROM ATOMS?

1. Gallup, "Evolution, Creationism, Intelligent Design," 2014, http://www.gallup.com/poll/21814/evolution-creationism-intelligent-design.aspx.

2. Forsthoefel, *Religious Faith Meets Modern Science*, ix.

3. David P. Barash, "God, Darwin and My College Biology Class," *New York Times*, September 27, 2014.

4. Douglas L. T. Rohde, Steve Olson, and Joseph T. Chan, "Modelling the Recent Common Ancestry of All Living Humans," *Nature* 431 (September 30, 2004): 562–565.

5. James P. Noonan, "Neanderthal Genomics and the Evolution of Modern Humans," *Genome Research* 20 (May 2010): 547–553.

6. *OED Online*, s.v. "molecular clock," accessed March 12, 2016, http://www.oed.com/view/Entry/252600.

7. Brown, et al., 393.

8. Ibid., 393.

9. Voet and Voet, *Biochemistry*, 19–24.

10. Alton Biggs, Kathleen Gregg, Whitney Crispen Hagins, Chris Kapicka, Linda Lundgren, Peter Rillero, and National Geographic Society, *Biology: The Dynamics of Life* (Columbus, OH: Glencoe/McGraw Hill, 2002), 388.

11. Ibid., 389.

12. Voet and Voet, *Biochemistry*, 21.

13. Ernst Mayr, *The Growth of Biological Thought: Diversity, Evolution, and Inheritance* (Cambridge, MA: The Belknap Press of Harvard University Press, 1982), 582.

14. Voet and Voet, *Biochemistry*, 19.

15. Alton Briggs, Kathleen Gregg, Whitney Crispen Hagins, Chris Kapicka, Linda Lundgren, Peter Rillero, National Geographic Society, *Biology: The Dynamics of Life* (Columbus, OH: Glencoe/McGraw-Hill, 2002), 389.

16. Donald Voet, Judith Voet, and Charlotte Pratt, *Fundamentals of Biochemistry: Life at the Molecular Level* (Hoboken, NJ: John Wiley and Sons, 2013), 2.

17. Voet and Voet, *Biochemistry*, 21.

18. Dorothy M. C. Hodgkin, "John Desmond Bernal 1901–1971," *Biographical Memoirs of the Fellows of the Royal Society* 26 (December 1980): 63.

19. Voet and Voet, *Biochemistry*, 21.

20. Sidney W. Fox, et al. "Experimental Retracement of the Origins of a Proto-cell: It Was Also a Protoneuron," *Journal of Biological Physics* 20 (1994): 17–36.

21. Steen Rasmussen, Mark A. Bedau, Liaohai Chen, David Deamer, David C. Krakauer, Norman H. Packard, and Peter F. Stadler, eds. *Protocells: Bridging Nonliving and Living Matter* (Cambridge: Massachusetts Institute of Technology, 2009), 125; Robert M. Hazen, *Genesis: The Scientific Quest for Life's Origins* (Washington, DC: Joseph Henry Press, 2005), 158.

22. John C. Priscu, "Origin and Evolution of Life on a Frozen Earth: Scientists Debate Whether Life's Start Was Hot or Cold," National Science Foundation Flash Special Report, accessed December 5, 2015, http://www.nsf.gov/news/special_reports/darwin/textonly/polar_essay1.jsp.

8. ARE CREATIONISM AND INTELLIGENT DESIGN CORRECT?

1. Victor P. Warkulwiz, *The Doctrines of Genesis 1–11: A Compendium and Defense of Traditional Catholic Theology on Origins: Everything a Catholic needs to know to uphold the literal truth of Genesis 1–11* (New York: iUniverse, 2007).

2. Ibid., 8.

3. Ibid.

4. Ibid.

5. Ibid., 10.

6. Stephen C. Meyer, "Intelligent Design Is Not Creationism," *The Daily Telegraph*, February 9, 2006.

7. William Dembski, *The Design Revolution: Answering the Toughest Questions about Intelligent Design* (Nottingham, UK: Inter-Varsity Press, 2004), Preface.

8. Meyer, "Intelligent Design Is Not Creationism," 2006.

9. Ibid.

10. Dembski, *Design Revolution*, chap. 20.

11. Ibid., 152–153.

12. Ibid., 152.

13. Ibid., 153.

14. Ibid., 152.

15. Ibid., 153.

16. Ibid.

17. *OED Online*, s.v. "create," accessed March 12, 2016, http://www.oed.com/view/Entry/44061.

18. Aquinas, *Works* 13:21 (*Summa Theologiæ* I.2.3).

9. CAN A CHRISTIAN ACCEPT THE THEORY OF EVOLUTION?

1. Ewen Callaway, "Modern Human Genomes Reveal Our Inner Neanderthal Ancestor" *Nature News*, January 29, 2014, http://www.nature.com/news/modern-human-genomes-reveal-our-inner-neanderthal-1.14615.

2. Sriram Sankararaman, Nick Patterson, Heng Li, Svante Pääbo, David Reich, "The Date of Interbreeding between Neandertals and Modern Humans," *PLOS Genetics* (October 4, 2012).

3. Ibid.

4. Ott, *Fundamentals of Catholic Dogma*, 92.

5. *OED Online*, s.v. "real" and "actual," accessed March 13, 2016, http://www.oed.com/view/Entry/158926 and http://www.oed.com/view/Entry/1972.

6. Ibid., s.v. "literal," accessed March 13, 2016, http://www.oed.com/view/Entry/109055.

7. Ott, *Fundamentals of Catholic Dogma*, 94.

8. Ibid.

9. Ibid., 95.

10. Ibid.

11. *OED Online*, s.v. "immediate," accessed March 13, 2016, http://www.oed.com/view/Entry/91838.

12. Ott, *Fundamentals of Catholic Dogma*, 95.

13. Ibid., 96.

14. Pius XII, *Humani Generis* [Concerning Some False Opinions Threatening to Undermine the Foundations of Catholic Doctrine] (Vatican City: Libreria Editrice Vaticana, 1950), 36, http://w2.vatican.va/content/pius-xii/en/encyclicals/documents/hf_p-xii_enc_12081950_humani-generis.html.

15. Ott, *Fundamentals of Catholic Dogma*, 99.

16. Ibid., 100.

17. Pius XII, *Humani Generis*, 36.

18. Ott, *Fundamentals of Catholic Dogma*, 95.

19. Ibid., 96.

20. Forsthoefel, *Religious Faith Meets Modern Science*, 31.

21. Augustine, *Sancti Aureli Augustini de Genesi ad litteram libri duodecim*, J. Zycha, ed., in *Corpus Scriptorum Ecclesiasticorum Latinorum*, vol. XXVIII, sec. III, pt. 1 (Vienna: F. Tempsky, 1894), bk. I, chap. 19, 28–29; quoted in translation to English in Jaki, *Science and Creation*, 182.

22. Augustine, *De Genesi*, bk. II, chap. 10, 47; quoted in translation to English in Jaki, *Science and Creation*, 183.

23. Charles Darwin, *The Origin of Species: By Means of Natural Selection of the Preservation of Favoured Races in the Struggle for Life* (New York: Signet Classics, 1958), chap. 1.

24. Martin A. Nowak and Roger Highfield, *Super Cooperators: Altruism, Evolution, and Why We Need Each Other to Succeed* (New York: Free Press, 2011).

25. Ibid., 10.

26. Forsthoefel, *Religious Faith Meets Modern Science*, chap. 8.

27. Ibid., 56–57.

28. Ibid.

29. Ibid., 57–59.

30. Ibid., 58–59.

31. Ibid.

32. Ibid., 60.

33. Ibid., 60–62.

34. Ibid., 60–61.

35. Ibid., 62–65.

36. Ibid., 63.

37. Ibid., 64.

38. Theodosius Dobzhansky, "Nothing in Biology Makes Sense Except in the Light of Evolution," *The American Biology Teacher* 35, no. 3 (March 1973): 125–129.

39. Qiaomei Fu et al., "An Early Modern Human from Romania with a Recent Neanderthal Ancestor," *Nature* 524 (June 2015): 216–219.

40. Rebecca L. Cann, Mark Stoneking, and Allan C. Wilson, "Mitochondrial DNA and Human Evolution," *Nature* 325 (January 1987): 31–36.

41. Naoyuki Takahata, "Allelic Genealogy and Human Evolution," *Molecular Biology and Evolution* 10, no. 1 (1993): 2–22; M. H. Wolpoff, "Multiregional Evolution: The Fossil Alternative to Eden," in *The Human Revolution: Behavioural and Biological Perspectives on the Origins of Modern Humans*, eds. P. Mellars and C. Stringer (Edinburgh: Edinburgh Press, 1989), chap. 6.

42. S. Zimmerman, "Population Size at the Time of Mitochondrial Eve," *Human Evolution* 16, no. 2 (April 2001): 117–124.

43. John C. Avise, Joseph E. Neigel, and Jonathan Arnold, "Demographic Influences on Mitochondrial DNA Lineage Survivorship in Animal Populations," *Journal of Molecular Evolution* 20 (1984): 99–105. "This may have occurred, but the results of

our models indicate that a dramatic population reduction does not necessarily have to be invoked to account for the human mtDNA data, even if all living humans have indeed descended from a recent female parent."

44. M. F. Hammer, "A Recent Common Ancestor for Human Y Chromosome," *Nature* 378 (November 1995): 376–378.

45. L. Simon Whitfield, Robin Lovell-Badge, and Peter N. Goodfellow, "Rapid Sequence Evolution of the Mammalian Sex-Determining Gene SRY," *Nature* 364 (August 1993): 713–716.

46. Hammer, "A Recent Common Ancestor for Human Y Chromosome," 376–378.

47. Ibid.

48. Paolo Francalacci, "Low-Pass DNA Sequencing of 1200 Sardinians Reconstructs European Y-Chromosome Phylogeny," *Science* 341 (August 2013): 565–569.

49. Yves Coppens, "Hominid Evolution and the Emergence of the Genus *Homo*," in *Neurosciences and the Human Person: New Perspectives on Human Activities, Scripta Varia* 121 (Vatican City: Pontifical Academy of Sciences, 2013).

50. Ibid., 1.

51. Ibid., 12.

52. Ray Kurzweil, *The Singularity Is Near: When Humans Transcend Biology* (New York: Penguin Group, 2005).

10. WHEN DOES A HUMAN LIFE BEGIN?

1. Gonzalo Herranz, "The Timing of Monozygotic Twinning: A Criticism of the Common Model," *Zygote* 23, no. 1 (February 2015): 27–40; online, June 5, 2013.

2. John M. Goldenring, "The Brain-Life Theory: Towards a Consistent Biological Definition," *Journal of Medical Ethics* 11 (December 1985): 198–204.

3. Ibid.

4. Scott F. Gilbert, *Developmental Biology*, 9th ed. (Sunderland, MA: Sinauer Associates, 2010), chapter 4.

5. Scott F. Gilbert, "When Does Human Life Begin?" originally on the companion website to *Developmental Biology*, 8th ed. The essay can be found here, accessed December 5, 2015, http://science.jburroughs.org/mbahe/BioEthics/Articles/When-doeshumanlifebegin.pdf.

6. Scott F. Gilbert, "When Does Human Personhood Begin," companion website to *Developmental Biology*, 10th ed., accessed December 5, 2015, http://10e.devbio.com/article.php?ch=1&id=312.

7. Scott F. Gilbert, "When Does Human Life Begin?" talk given to the American Reproductive Health Professional Society in 2010, recording found here (3:14), accessed March 14, 2016, http://www.swarthmore.edu/news-events/when-does-personhood-begin.

8. *OED Online*, s.v. "conception," accessed February 28, 2016, http://www.oed. com/view/Entry/38137.

9. Flannery O'Connor to "A.," 6 September 1955, in *The Habit of Being*, ed. Sally Fitzgerald (New York: Farrar, Straus and Giroux, 1979), 100.

Stacy A. Trasancos is a Catholic writer, scientist, teacher, and editor. She earned a bachelor's degree in science from East Texas State University, a doctorate in chemistry from Penn State University and a master's degree in dogmatic theology (summa cum laude) from Holy Apostles College and Seminary. She worked as research chemist for DuPont before becoming a full-time homemaker in 2003. Trasancos designed and was editor-in-chief of *Ignitum Today* (2011–2014) and serves as editor emeritus of *Catholic Stand*, which she cofounded. She is a contributor to *Integrated Catholic Life* and *Strange Notions*. Trasancos is an adjunct professor at Seton Hall University and at Holy Apostles, where she also serves as alumni association president. She teaches chemistry and physics classes at Kolbe Academy, where she also serves as department chair. She is the author of *Science Was Born of Christianity: The Teaching of Fr. Stanley L. Jaki.* Trasancos is a board member for the Institute for Theological Encounter with Science and Technology (ITEST) and a member of the Fellowship of Catholic Scholars.

She and her husband, José, have seven children and three grandchildren and live in the Adirondack mountains in New York.

AVE

AVE MARIA PRESS

Founded in 1865, Ave Maria Press,
a ministry of the Congregation of
Holy Cross, is a Catholic publishing
company that serves the spiritual and
formative needs of the Church and its
schools, institutions, and ministers;
Christian individuals and families; and
others seeking spiritual nourishment.

For a complete listing of titles from

Ave Maria Press

Sorin Books

Forest of Peace

Christian Classics

visit www.avemariapress.com

AVE MARIA PRESS
Notre Dame, IN
A Ministry of the United States Province of Holy Cross